10-MINUTE

BRAIN TEASERS

Dr. Gareth Moore is the author of a wide range of puzzle books for both adults and children. He gained his PhD at Cambridge University in the field of machine intelligence, later using his experience in computer software research and development to help produce the first book of Kakuro puzzles published in the UK. He has a wide range of media interests and also works on several puzzle and other Web sites, including his own www.dokakuro.com, www.dosudoku.com, www.dohanjie.com.

Also by Dr. Gareth Moore: *The Book of Kakuro, The Book of Japanese Puzzles, The Book of Hanjie, Quick Kakuro, The Kids' Book of Number Puzzles, The Kids' Book of Sudoku: Challenge Edition, The Kids' Book of Hanjie, The Kids' Book of Kakuro, The Book of Hitori, The Kids' Book of Hitori, Kids' 10-Minute Brain Workout, The Essential Book of Japanese Puzzles, The Essential Book of Hanje, The Essential Book of Kakuro, The Essential Book of Kakuro 2, Sudoku Makes You Smarter, The Rough Guide Book of Brain Training, The Little Book of Sudoku Volume Four, Slitherlink, Keep Your Brain Fit: 101 Ways to Tone Your Mind, The Mammoth Book of Brain Workouts, Train the Brain, Killer Sudoku, Sudoku Xtra Issue 1, Sudoku Xtra Issue 2, Sudoku Xtra Issue 3, Sudoku Xtra Issue 4, Sudoku 25x25 Volume 1, Sudoku 16x16 Volume 1, Hard-As-Nails Sudoku Volume Five,* and the forthcoming *Solve This!: Word Puzzles* and *Solve This!: Number Logic.*

10-MINUTE BRAIN TEASERS

Brain-Training Tips, Logic Tests, and Puzzles to Exercise Your Mind

Gareth Moore

SKYHORSE PUBLISHING

Skyhorse Publishing books may be purchased in bulk at special discounts for sales promotion, corporate gifts, fund-raising, or educational purposes. Special editions can also be created to specifications. For details, contact the Special Sales Department, Skyhorse Publishing, 555 Eighth Avenue, Suite 903, New York, NY 10018 or info@skyhorsepublishing.com.

www.skyhorsepublishing.com

10 9 8 7 6 5 4 3 2 1

Library of Congress Cataloging-in-Publication Data

Moore, Gareth, 1975-
  10-minute brain teasers: brain-training tips, logic tests, and puzzles to exercise your mind / Gareth Moore.
    p. cm.
  ISBN 978-1-60239-345-5 (pbk. : alk. paper)
  1. Puzzles. 2. Logic puzzles. 3. Lateral thinking puzzles. I. Title II. Title: Ten-minute.
  GV1493.M55 2010
  793.73--dc22
                                            2010013351

Printed in China

Contents

The Ten-Minute Brain Workout

We all know that physical exercise is important for maintaining our general health and well-being, but what's less widely known is that mental exercise is equally important for maintaining our brains. Exercising your body on a regular basis improves muscle tone, increasing the flow of blood and so improving the delivery of oxygen and nutrients to your muscles. Similarly, your brain requires exercise to ensure the maintenance of the all-important inter-neural connections within. This book is specially designed to help with exactly this kind of exercise—it contains ninety days of ten-minute exercises that will help you build up your brain to keep it fit and healthy. And what's more, you'll have fun doing it!

Different types of mental challenge work different parts of your brain, just as different types of exercise work different muscles in your body. At a gym you can choose from a range of exercise machines and weights programs that are designed to target specific muscle groups, or alternatively you can go swimming or join an aerobics class where you will be exercising many more muscles for a much more comprehensive workout. Research has shown that, in this respect, the brain is remarkably similar. Focusing on a single problem or task for a lengthy period of time tends to use only a small part of the brain, while working through a series of shorter but more varied tasks uses much more of it. That's where *10-Minute Brain Teasers* comes in—it's packed full of a mix of different puzzles, challenges, and observation and memory tests. Each page has a task or set of tasks that should take you no more than ten minutes, but will quite probably contribute more to your general mental well-being than a whole day of focusing on a single problem.

But why should we force ourselves to use larger areas of our brains if we don't really need to? Again, you can compare using more of your brain to using more of your body in an aerobics session—you need to exercise as much of your brain as you can in order to keep the whole thing fit and healthy. Just as your body begins to lose its strength and agility as you grow older, so the general effect of aging on the brain is for it to become less supple and to start to lose its strength. Just consider that there are around one hundred billion neurons in your brain—neurons are the brain cells that, among other things, control the main cognitive functions of language, attention, reasoning, memory, and visual and spatial awareness. On top of this there are around one hundred to five hundred *trillion* connections between them, called synapses. Each neuron is linked to between one thousand and twenty-five thousand others by these synapses, which act like electrical wiring between the active components of a hugely complex computer. Unlike a computer, however, synapses will fade and die if they are not used. A three-year-old child has one thousand trillion synapses, with at least half having gone by adulthood. A good brain workout will help prevent further decline.

The general effect of regular brain exercise is to improve the memory, to sharpen the mind, and to slow down the whole process of mental decay. Exercise, however, is not the only requirement for a fit and healthy brain. Just as you need a healthy regime to maintain a healthy body, so the same is true of your brain. Sleep is one of the key factors in keeping your brain in top form. Proper rest is every bit as important as proper exercise, but sleeping well is not always as easy as we might hope.

Every aspect of your lifestyle is linked in almost as many ways as the neurons in your brain. Many factors can interfere with sleep, but looking after yourself properly is a critically important step. Falling into bed at midnight having spent the entire evening drinking in a smoke-filled pub before tucking into a greasy hamburger on the way home is not the way to achieve restful sleep—especially if you know you will have to be awake again in a few hours to go to work. Although some people can manage perfectly well with less, most of us need at least seven to eight hours of sleep each night. If you find it difficult to get to sleep, you may need to look at a variety of things that can conspire to keep you awake. Eating late at night or drinking common stimulants such as tea, coffee, or fizzy drinks with a high caffeine content can make it harder to sleep.

Although you might think that drinking alcohol helps you to relax, and may well help you to fall asleep, heavy drinking is not the best way to achieve a good night's rest! The detrimental effects of overdrinking are quite horrific. Small amounts of alcohol cause chemical imbalances in the brain that affect our thought patterns and comprehension, as well as impairing our speech, balance, and general motor functions. A larger intake of alcohol consistent with alcohol abuse over a long period can make your brain shrink, damage the frontal lobes, and cause a whole catalogue of other health problems.

It probably comes as no surprise that the healthiest thing you can drink is fresh water. Our blood is eighty-five percent water and drinking between six and eight glasses of fresh, clean water every day helps to ensure toxins are flushed from our system, improving energy levels and general concentration. The brain relies on the blood to deliver the oxygen and various amino acids it needs to function properly. Drinking too little water will also cause dehydration that can significantly impair the brain's performance.

Another major factor in inhibiting brain power is smoking. Smoking reduces the supply of oxygen to the brain and depletes the body's B vitamins, which are vital for mental energy. The general health hazards involved in smoking are well known, but it is something of a myth that smoking helps you to concentrate, despite what committed smokers may think. Because of the reduction in the oxygen supply, smoking actually impairs brain function.

As a rule, those things that are bad for your general well-being are also bad for your brain, but luckily there are also plenty of things that help keep your brain in good health. For example, eating oily fish as part of your diet is very good for your brain. Mackerel, salmon, trout, herring, sardines, and tuna are all rich in Omega-3 fatty acids. The brain is mostly water, but sixty percent of the solid part is fat and needs a regular supply of Omega-3s.

Other foods that are good for your brain include raw broccoli. Broccoli is full of vitamins, making it a particularly healthy food, but it also contains glutathione, an antioxidant that protects brain cells from what is known as "oxidative stress," which can destroy the cells. Foods that are rich in beta-carotene, which the body converts to the essential antioxidant vitamin A, are also good for your brain. These include fresh carrots, sweet potatoes, and most dark green vegetables.

Fresh lean meat, chicken, and eggs are all good sources of proteins that increase the level of the amino acid tyrosine in your bloodstream. This encourages the brain to produce the adrenalin derivative norepinephrine, improving memory, alertness, and concentration. Dopamine will be produced as well, and this is associated with coordination and muscle control. Nuts are also full of protein, with almonds being especially good for the brain as they also contain valuable minerals and Omega-6 fatty acids.

There are many other foods that are good for the brain. Most fruit is full of vitamins, and bananas are another excellent source of tyrosine. Beans such as soy beans, red beans, or black beans are rich in protein and minerals, although these beans do need to be cooked properly to destroy the toxins they contain. It is safe to say that eating a varied, well-balanced diet, eating regular meals (especially breakfast), and limiting your intake of processed food or junk food will help to keep your brain in good condition just as it helps to keep your body in shape.

The exercises in *10-Minute Brain Teasers* will go some way towards improving your brain fitness, but there are many other forms of mental exercise that you can incorporate into your daily routine. In fact, varying your daily routine will help to keep your mind alert, keep you thinking about what you are doing instead of drifting along "on automatic pilot," and keep your brain active. You can start from the moment you get up in the morning simply by brushing your teeth or eating your cereal with the other hand. On the way to a regular destination such as work, why not try getting off the bus a stop or two early and walking the rest of the way, or taking a different route altogether?

Hobbies that make you concentrate in a way that is different from the way you focus on your usual work are also good for activating different areas of the brain. Chess, card games like bridge, jigsaw puzzles, or even knitting all provide a bit of mental exercise, as do sports such as tennis or golf, which also improve coordination and general fitness. Maintaining a reasonable level of physical fitness will always help in improving blood circulation, and your brain likes nothing better than a healthy flow of blood. Walking, swimming, and jogging are all good forms of physical exercise that can be combined with a mental workout, such as thinking of a long word, like "acceleration," and then seeing how many anagrams or other words you can make from it.

Regularly learning new words is a good way to improve your memory. You could even keep a dictionary by your bed and learn a new word every morning when you get up. Learning a foreign language is another way of keeping your powers of recall up to scratch, research having shown that mastering a foreign tongue can provide significant protection against short- and long-term memory loss.

Even if you already have all aspects of your physical and mental exercise regime fully under control, it doesn't mean to say that you won't benefit from *10-Minute Brain Teasers*. At the very least, it is a pleasant way to pass a few minutes once a day.

All the puzzles in the book are designed to be fair. They don't require you to guess, and they don't require you to spend an enormous amount of time on them. What they do require you to do is to think logically about the problems in front of you. If it's a puzzle, then think about what deductions you can make, or if it's a memory test, then think about how you might go about remembering what you need to remember. If it involves any math and it looks complex, then think about how you can simplify it—where there are particularly nasty-looking math problems in this book, they virtually always have an easy route. In fact, many of them are specifically designed to make you read the whole question and think first. For example, multiplying by 582 might be tricky, but if the next step is to divide by 582, then it really isn't very hard at all!

Ten minutes is a target, but on many of the tests you may be able to beat this. On others you might find that ten minutes isn't long enough for you, in which case you may choose to have fun completing the puzzle and take as long as you like, or come back to it for another ten-minute trial at some point in the future. Don't worry if you seem to be taking a long time on a test—for some of the types, such as sudoku, the length of time you take will very much depend on how experienced you are at solving this type of puzzle.

The structure of the book is such that all the puzzles and other content become harder as you progress, as well as being broken down into three distinct levels—Beginners, Advanced, and Expert. Each page of questions or puzzles is followed by another page with the solutions or, in the case of the memory tests, with some empty boxes to fill in with what you remember. The idea is that you should do a page of puzzles or questions every day. Of course, there's nothing stopping you from using the book in any way you want. As long as you use the book regularly, then you'll be getting the benefit of the brain workout.

Every page contains instructions, but if you're confused about how to solve one of the puzzles, then take a quick peek at the next page to see what an example solution looks like—it won't help you work out *why* it's the answer, so you'll still have just as much challenge involved in solving it, even if you can remember parts of the answer when you flick back.

Without spoiling any surprises about the types of puzzle and questions you'll encounter in the book, a few general tips could still be useful. First, remember to think logically about everything. The puzzles and tests are designed to make you *think*, so if you're sometimes stuck, then that's not necessarily a bad thing! If the question has numbers and units in it, such as miles per hour, then think about what the unit actually is—"miles per hour" effectively means "miles divided by hours," so if you're told a train traveled at 40 mph for 15 minutes, then that means "miles divided by hours equals 40," or put another way, "40 times hours equals miles." In a quarter of an hour, therefore, it went 0.25 (hours) times 40 equals 10 miles. Just a little bit of logical thought about the question will usually make even the toughest-looking problem simple to answer.

Secondly, if it's a memory test, then try building mental pictures in your head. These force you to think and process what you are reading, and if you make them ridiculous, then they can be memorable in their own right. For example, if you need to remember "bicycle" and "house," then imagine a bicycle flying over a house and you probably won't forget that association. You can build up long chains of imagery such as this and remember a surprisingly large amount of material. Even if you forget it, you'll be making your brain work so you'll still be getting the benefit—and the practice will help improve your memory!

Finally, don't be afraid to make notes of what you've worked out so far. You'll need a pencil to write in some of the answers anyway, so you might as well use it as you go. Of course, if you can keep everything in your head, then so much the better; but if you find yourself glazing over or you find that it's taking too long, then just write things out as you go—it usually helps clarify your thoughts. With some of the puzzles, such as kakuro or sudoku, writing things out can also be an invaluable shortcut.

If you use this book for just ten minutes every day, then the workout your brain receives could be an important part of maintaining your general health and well-being. Research has shown that just this small amount of regular brain exercise can make elderly people as sharp and alert as people ten years younger than they. No matter how old you are, your brain is so important to everything you do that you really owe it to yourself to keep it in shape. *10-Minute Brain Teasers* will help you to do just that.

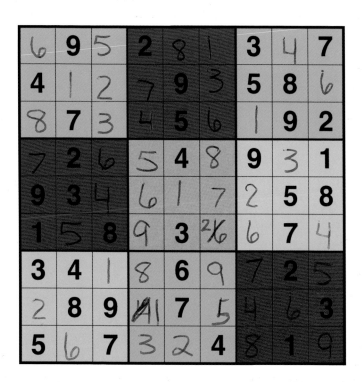

Sudoku

Sudoku has one very simple rule: fill in the grid so that each row, column, and marked 3 by 3 box contains each of the numbers 1 to 9 once and once only.

No guessing is required, and there is only one solution. If you're not sure you understand the rules, then take a quick peek at the answer to see how it works.

6	9	5	2	8	1	3	4	7
4	1	2	7	9	3	5	8	6
8	7	3	4	5	6	1	9	2
7	2	6	5	4	8	9	3	1
9	3	4	6	1	7	2	5	8
1	5	8	9	3	2	6	7	4
3	4	1	8	6	9	7	2	5
2	8	9	1	7	5	4	6	3
5	6	7	3	2	4	8	1	9

Read this tale of tails, and then answer as many questions as you can without checking the text again. Then when you've done that, go back and check the text and answer the rest.

On Tuesdays, Katie tends to go for a walk in the park with her brother Tom's dog, Sammy. Sammy is quite a friendly dog and so tends to say hello in a doggy kind of way to quite a mix of canine chums. Particular friends of Sammy include Woof, the golden retriever owned by the local barber, and Mr. Bark, the small spaniel that's frequently found yapping madly at small children who dare to come into his domain. Sammy is a creature of habit, so he tends to walk Katie around the park in a clockwise direction, while the other dogs take their owners around the circular park path in a counter-clockwise direction. Sometimes the barber, Bob, walks his dog in the same direction as Sammy, but truth be told, he generally only does this on Wednesdays. Odd but true.

Occasionally, a neighborhood cat has the temerity to wander across what is clearly Sammy's own turf on earth, and, in fact, Katie's tortoiseshell cat Black sometimes also does this—although usually she knows better than to do this on Tuesdays. But the funny thing is that, on other days of the week, she only wanders in when there's the chance to try and bully the window cleaner's little yappy spaniel that isn't quite so brave as his yappy little mouth would like you to think. Friday's good for that.

This cat and dog life has been going on for the best part of three years now, so maybe it's time for things to change—Sammy's even considering walking the other way around the park now! Of course if he did that he'd bump into his doggy friends/foes not quite so often, so he's not sure; he might only do that on alternate Tuesdays.

- Which way around the park does Mr. Bark walk?
- On what days of the week do we know the barber is in the park?
- What color is Black?
- What job does the spaniel's owner have?
- What is the relationship between Katie and Tom?
- Which dogs sometimes or always walk clockwise around the park?
- How many different people are mentioned by name?
- How many times is the word "chum" (or chums) used in this story?
- On what day of the week does the cat in the story normally avoid the park?
- What sort of dog is Woof?
- If Sammy walked the other way around the park, how often is he planning to do this?
- How many rabbits co-star in this story?

Which way around the park does Mr. Bark walk?
Counter-clockwise.

On what days of the week do we know the barber is in the park?
Tuesday and Wednesday.

What color is Black?
Tortoiseshell.

What job does the spaniel's owner have?
Window cleaner.

What is the relationship between Katie and Tom?
Siblings. (Tom is Katie's brother.)

Which dogs sometimes or always walk clockwise around the park?
Sammy and Woof.

How many different people are mentioned by name?
Three.

How many times is the word "chum" (or chums) used in this story?
Just the once.

On what day of the week does the cat in the story normally avoid the park?
Tuesday.

What sort of dog is Woof?
Golden retriever.

If Sammy walked the other way around the park, how often is he planning to do this?
On alternate Tuesdays.

How many rabbits co-star in this story?
Absolutely none!

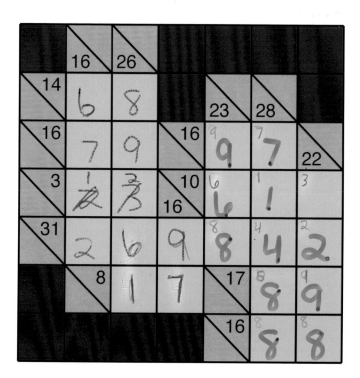

Kakuro

Fill in the grid so that each run of squares adds up to the total in the box above or to the left. You can only use the numbers 1 to 9, and you may not repeat any number within any run (a number may reoccur in the same row/column in a separate run). Totals below the diagonal line give the sum of the numbers in the run below, while totals to the right of the diagonal line give the sum of numbers in the run to the right.

No guessing is required, and there is only one solution. If you're not sure you understand the rules, then take a quick peek at the answer to see how it works.

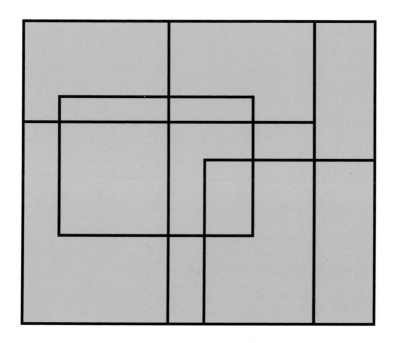

- How many clear corners (┐┘└┌) are there in this illustration? 2O
- How many rectangles can you count? 16
- How many different colors would you need to color in each shape so that no two colors were adjacent to one another? 3
- How many intersections are there where a "+" sign is formed? 8
- And how many intersections where a "T" is formed? 3

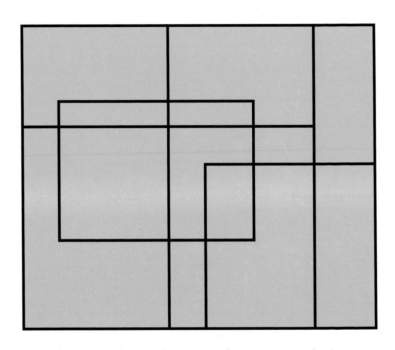

How many clear corners (˥˩˪˻) are there in this illustration?
9.

How many rectangles can you count?
There are at least 26.

How many different colors would you need to color in each shape so that no two colors were adjacent to one another?
3.

How many intersections are there where a "+" sign is formed?
8.

And how many intersections where a "T" is formed?
8.

Which of these words is the odd one out, and why?
Italy   France   Paris   Spain   Germany

Which number comes next in this sequence?
7   9   11   13   ?   *15*

Fire engine is to fire station as ambulance is to?   *Hospital*

Which of these numbers would look the same if viewed upside down?
123   765   906   938

How many minutes are there in 5 hours?   *300*

If my normal 30-minute journey somehow takes me 45 minutes today, and I normally drive at 45 mph, how fast did I drive today?   *52 mph*

If the temperature rises from 6°C to 17°C, by how many degrees Celsius has it risen?   *11*

Complete the following:
12 x 2 = ?   96 − 4 = ?   5 x 3 = ?   *24   24   15*

True or false? A ton of feathers weighs more than a ton of steel.   *False*

Which letter comes next in this pattern?
A B A B A ?   *B*

Complete the following:
123 + 5 = ?   9 ÷ 3 = ?   27 − 12 = ?   *128   3   15*

If I press the button "2" on my mobile phone I select A, then B, then C. How many times do I need to press "2" to type "CAB"?   *6 times*

Which of these words is not a palindrome? (A palindrome is a word or phrase that reads the same both forwards and backwards.)
Dad   Mom   Son   Bob

If three people go to the park but only two leave the park, how many people remain in the park?

1 person

Which of these words is the odd one out, and why?

Italy   France   Paris   Spain   Germany

Paris—only one that isn't a country.

Which number comes next in this sequence?

7   9   11   13   ?

15.

Fire engine is to fire station as ambulance is to?

Hospital.

Which of these numbers would look the same if viewed upside down?

123   765   906   938

906.

How many minutes are there in 5 hours?

300 minutes.

If my normal 30-minute journey somehow takes me 45 minutes today, and I normally drive at 45 mph, how fast did I drive today?

30 mph.

If the temperature rises from 6°C to 17°C, by how many degrees Celsius has it risen?

11°C.

Complete the following:

$12 \times 2 = ?$ $96 - 4 = ?$ $5 \times 3 = ?$

$12 \times 2 = 24$ $96 - 4 = 92$ $5 \times 3 = 15$

True or false? A ton of feathers weighs more than a ton of steel.

False. They both weigh a ton.

Which letter comes next in this pattern?

A B A B A ?

B.

Complete the following:

$123 + 5 = ?$ $9 \div 3 = ?$ $27 - 12 = ?$

$123 + 5 = 128$ $9 \div 3 = 3$ $27 - 12 = 15$

If I press the button "2" on my mobile phone I select A, then B, then C. How many times do I need to press "2" to type "CAB"?

6 times.

Which of these words is not a palindrome? (A palindrome is a word or phrase that reads the same both forwards and backwards.)

Dad   Mom   Son   Bob

Son.

If three people go to the park but only two leave the park, how many people remain in the park?

One.

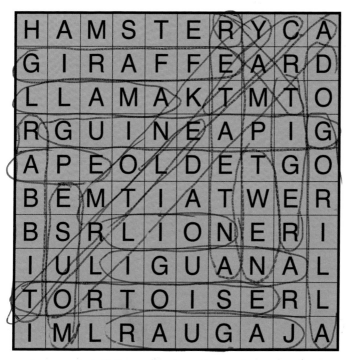

H	A	M	S	T	E	R	Y	C	A
G	I	R	A	F	F	E	A	R	D
L	L	A	M	A	K	T	M	T	O
R	G	U	I	N	E	A	P	I	G
A	P	E	O	L	D	E	T	G	O
B	E	M	T	I	A	T	W	E	R
B	S	R	L	I	O	N	E	R	I
I	U	L	I	G	U	A	N	A	L
T	O	R	T	O	I	S	E	R	L
I	M	L	R	A	U	G	A	J	A

See if you can find all the animals that are camouflaged within this grid.

ANTEATER   GUINEA PIG   MOUSE

APE   HAMSTER   NEWT

ARMADILLO   IGUANA   RABBIT

CAT   JAGUAR   RAT

DOG   LION   TIGER

GIRAFFE   LLAMA   TORTOISE

GORILLA   MONKEY   TURTLE

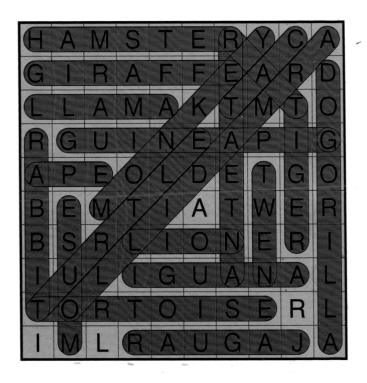

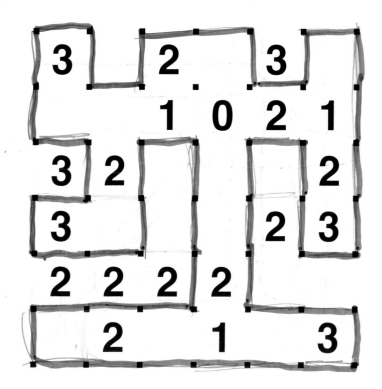

Slitherlink

Draw a single loop by connecting together the dots such that each numbered square has the specified number of adjacent line segments. You may only join dots by using straight horizontal or vertical lines, and the loop cannot cross or overlap itself in any way.

No guessing is required, and there is only one solution. If you're not sure you understand the rules, then take a quick peek at the answer to see how it works.

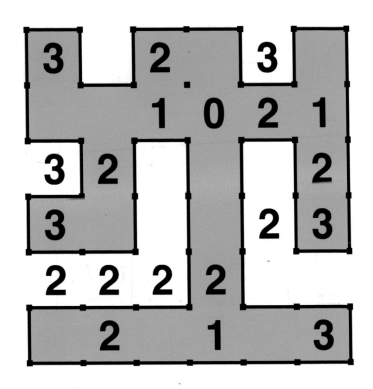

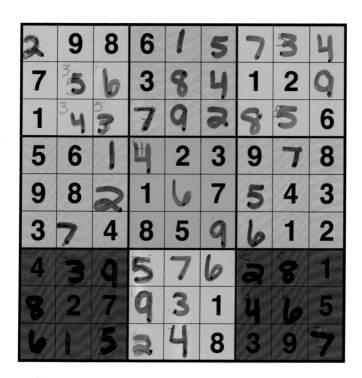

Sudoku

Sudoku has one very simple rule: fill in the grid so that each row, column, and marked 3 by 3 box contains each of the numbers 1 to 9 once and once only.

No guessing is required, and there is only one solution. If you're not sure you understand the rules, then take a quick peek at the answer to see how it works.

2	9	8	6	1	5	7	3	4
7	5	6	3	8	4	1	2	9
1	4	3	7	9	2	8	5	6
5	6	1	4	2	3	9	7	8
9	8	2	1	6	7	5	4	3
3	7	4	8	5	9	6	1	2
4	3	9	5	7	6	2	8	1
8	2	7	9	3	1	4	6	5
6	1	5	2	4	8	3	9	7

Memory Test

Spend a few minutes memorizing these fruits and which box they're in.

Then when you turn the page, you'll be asked to fill in the empty boxes in the same arrangement.

Apple	Pear	Banana	Satsuma
Orange	Peach	Cherry	Grape
Lychee	Pineapple	Date	Raspberry
Strawberry	Pomegranate	Elderberry	Watermelon

Now try and fill in the table without checking back to the previous page:

Apple	P EAR	B ANANA	Satsuma
Orange	P EAR	C HERRY	Grape
lychee	pine apple	D ATE	Rasberry
Strawberry	POME granite	EL DER BERRY	Water melon

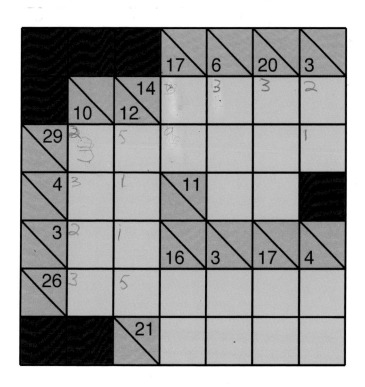

Kakuro

Fill in the grid so that each run of squares adds up to the total in the box above or to the left. You can only use the numbers 1 to 9, and you may not repeat any number within any run (a number may reoccur in the same row/column in a separate run). Totals below the diagonal line give the sum of the numbers in the run below, while totals to the right of the diagonal line give the sum of numbers in the run to the right.

No guessing is required, and there is only one solution. If you're not sure you understand the rules, then take a quick peek at the answer to see how it works.

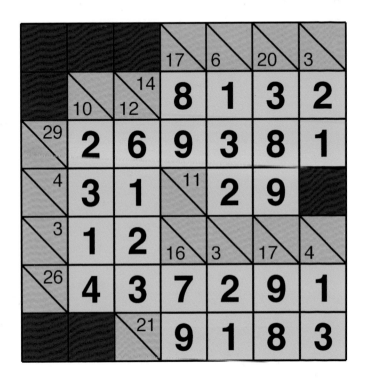

Which of these words is the odd one out, and why?
Tool   Heel   Baas   (Tale)   Keel

Which number comes next in this sequence?
19   15   11   7   ? *3*

Food is to eat as water is to? *Drink*

Which of these numbers would look the same if viewed in a mirror?
456   656   609   (808)

If it's 2:45 p.m. now, then what time will it be in two and a half hours? *5:15*

If Bob drives at 70 mph for 20 minutes, then 30 mph for 5 minutes, followed by 70 mph for 10 minutes, how long does his journey take?

If iron melts at 1538°C, copper melts at 1085°C, and silicon melts at 1414°C, which melts at the lowest temperature? *Copper*

Complete the following:
$5 + 5 + 5 = ?$ *15* $9 \times 3 = ?$ *27* $17 - 16 = ?$ *1*

True or false? If I'm 5 years younger than my friend, then he must be 5 years older than me. *True*

Which letter comes next in this pattern?
A C D A C D A C ? *D*

Complete the following:
$987 + 5 = ?$ *1002* $45 - 42 = ?$ *3* $13 \times 2 = ?$ *26*

How many button presses do I need to type the number 5,432,670 into my calculator? *6*

Which of these words is spelled incorrectly?
Uncle   Aunt   Son   (Dawter)

If I buy two bags of chips and give one away, then buy two more but eat one, how many full bas do I now have? *2*

Which of these words is the odd one out, and why?
Tool   Heel   Baas   Tale   Keel
Tale. It is the only one without a double letter in the middle.

Which number comes next in this sequence?
19   15   11   7   ?
3.

Food is to eat as water is to?
Drink.

Which of these numbers would look the same if viewed in a mirror?
456   656   609   808
808.

If it's 2:45 p.m. now, then what time will it be in two and a half hours?
5:15 p.m.

If Bob drives at 70 mph for 20 minutes, then 30 mph for 5 minutes, followed by 70 mph for 10 minutes, how long does his journey take?
It takes 35 minutes—the speeds are unimportant.

If iron melts at 1538°C, copper melts at 1085°C, and silicon melts at 1414°C, which melts at the lowest temperature?
Copper.

Complete the following:
5 + 5 + 5 = ?   9 x 3 = ?   17 – 16 = ?
5 + 5 + 5 = 15   9 x 3 = 27   17 – 16 = 1

True or false? If I'm 5 years younger than my friend, then he must be 5 years older than me.
True.

Which letter comes next in this pattern?
A C D A C D A C ?
D.

Complete the following:
987 + 5 = ?   45 – 42 = ?   13 x 2 = ?
987 + 5 = 992   45 – 42 = 3   13 x 2 = 26

How many button presses do I need to type the number 5,432,670 into my calculator?
7 button presses.

Which of these words is spelled incorrectly?
Uncle   Aunt   Son   Dawter
Dawter (daughter).

If I buy two bags of chips and give one away, then buy two more but eat one, how many full bags do I now have?
Two bags.

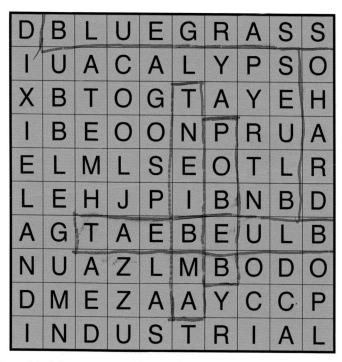

D	B	L	U	E	G	R	A	S	S
I	U	A	C	A	L	Y	P	S	O
X	B	T	O	G	T	A	Y	E	H
I	B	E	O	O	N	P	R	U	A
E	L	M	L	S	E	O	T	L	R
L	E	H	J	P	I	B	N	B	D
A	G	T	A	E	B	E	U	L	B
N	U	A	Z	L	M	B	O	D	O
D	M	E	Z	A	A	Y	C	C	P
I	N	D	U	S	T	R	I	A	L

Try and find these current and historical popular music styles within the grid.

AMBIENT

BEBOP

BLUEBEAT

BLUEGRASS

BLUES

BUBBLEGUM

CALYPSO

COOLJAZZ

COUNTRY

DEATHMETAL

DIXIELAND

DUB

GOSPEL

HARDBOP

INDUSTRIAL

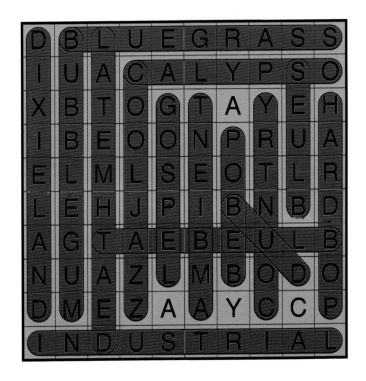

4	5	1	7	9	8	3	6	2
7	6	3	4	5	2	8	9	1
2	8	9	1	6	3	4	7	5
5	9	7	2	8	6	1	4	3
8	3	4	9	1	5	6	2	7
6	1	2	3	7	4	5	8	9
1	7	6	8	3	9	2	5	4
3	2	5	6	4	7	9	1	8
9	4	8	5	2	1	7	3	6

Sudoku

Sudoku has one very simple rule: fill in the grid so that each row, column, and marked 3 by 3 box contains each of the numbers 1 to 9 once and once only.

No guessing is required, and there is only one solution. If you're not sure you understand the rules, then take a quick peek at the answer to see how it works.

4	5	1	7	9	8	3	6	2
7	6	3	4	5	2	8	9	1
2	8	9	1	6	3	4	7	5
5	9	7	2	8	6	1	4	3
8	3	4	9	1	5	6	2	7
6	1	2	3	7	4	5	8	9
1	7	6	8	3	9	2	5	4
3	2	5	6	4	7	9	1	8
9	4	8	5	2	1	7	3	6

Read this odd diary entry and then answer as many questions as you can without checking the text again. Then when you've done that, go back and check the text and answer the rest.

On a cold day the wind blows from the northwest; on a warm day it often comes from the south. Today it's very cold, but the wind is still from the south. That's weird. It's not what I expect. I expect it to be consistent. But it isn't. The wind is a pain. But not as much as this rain. The rain is persistent, and when it's not I'm sure it's simply waiting; waiting to persist. It's been persistently raining since last week, or perhaps the week before that. Yes, it was the week before; since Tuesday two weeks ago. It hasn't been dry since. It's funny, really; until then I thought I wanted it to rain. I'm not so sure now. I've never really got on with the weather. The weather is like a word I can't quite spell. It teeters at the edge of my mind; if only I could think of the first letter I'm sure I'd work it out. But I never do. It's not like I can't spell, so why can't I get the weather right? If I did then the crops might grow better. I'd make more money. You never know; it could happen. I'd need less subsidies anyway. I don't like the subsidies. Well, I mean I like to have them, but I don't like that I do. You know what I mean. Anyway, I watch the TV weather, but that's no better. What do they know? They're not here in the country anyway. I see it blow in the tree; rain in the stream; gale in the night; die in the morning. It's always the morning when it goes quiet; it tempts you out of the house, like a hand of sugar to lead a horse—it's a deception. It isn't going to carry on like that; it just gets you on the way. Then it springs the usual trap. It lets flow with water and storm and lightning and—surely it must be summer soon? This winter is too long. The nights are too dark, and the mornings too short. The wind comes and goes, beating the house; a pugilist fighting against the bell of the weather vane on the church—it spins and spins and squeaks and squeaks and keeps me up all night. I should get double-glazing. That might sort it out. But even then I'd still hear the banging of the barn doors. Should fix those too. I don't like the wind. And it's coming from the wrong direction.

- Which way is the wind coming from today? **S**
- What is it that squeaks and keeps me awake? **WV**
- What might make me more money if the weather were more predictable? **Crops**
- What is weird about the wind today? **Coming from S**
- When has it been raining since? **Tues**
- What might make it quieter at night? **WV / BD**
- At what time of day does the weather normally improve?
- What writing task do I liken predicting the weather to?
- If my crops grew better, what might I need less of?
- How do I suggest leading a horse?
- What makes a banging sound at night? **BD**
- Which direction does the wind usually come from on warm days? **S**
- What have I never really got on with? **Fixing BD**
- How many times do I use the word "wind"? **5**

Which way is the wind coming from today?
The south.

What is it that squeaks and keeps me awake?
The weather vane.

What might make me more money if the weather were more predictable?
My crops.

What is weird about the wind today?
It normally comes from the northwest, not the south.

When has it been raining since?
Tuesday two weeks ago.

What might make it quieter at night?
Double-glazing.

At what time of day does the weather normally improve?
The morning.

What writing task do I liken predicting the weather to?
Spelling.

If my crops grew better, what might I need less of?
Subsidies.

How do I suggest leading a horse?
With sugar.

What makes a banging sound at night?
The barn doors.

Which direction does the wind usually come from on warm days?
The south.

What have I never really got on with?
The weather.

How many times do I use the word "wind"?
Five times.

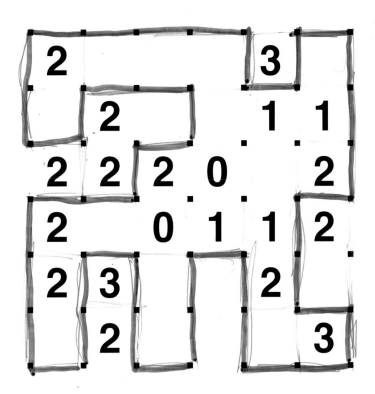

Slitherlink

Draw a single loop by connecting together the dots such that each numbered square has the specified number of adjacent line segments. You may only join dots by using straight horizontal or vertical lines, and the loop cannot cross or overlap itself in any way.

No guessing is required, and there is only one solution. If you're not sure you understand the rules, then take a quick peek at the answer to see how it works.

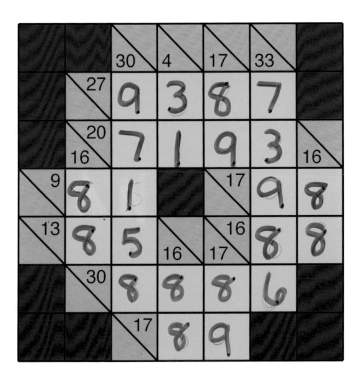

Kakuro

Fill in the grid so that each run of squares adds up to the total in the box above or to the left. You can only use the numbers 1 to 9, and you may not repeat any number within any run (a number may reoccur in the same row/column in a separate run). Totals below the diagonal line give the sum of the numbers in the run below, while totals to the right of the diagonal line give the sum of numbers in the run to the right.

No guessing is required, and there is only one solution. If you're not sure you understand the rules, then take a quick peek at the answer to see how it works.

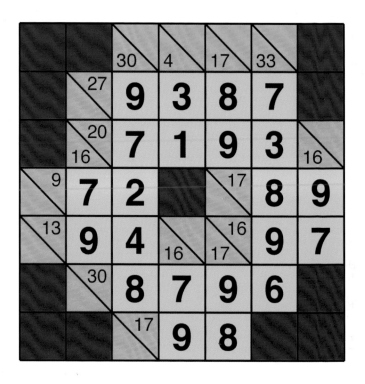

Which of these words is the odd one out, and why?
Train   Coach   (Truck)   Bus   Taxi

Which number comes next in this sequence?
2   4   8   16   ?   *32*

Airplane is to pilot as car is to? *Driver*

Which of these numbers gives the answer 9 if you add up all its individual digits?
123   456   (135)   247

How many hours are there in a weekend? *48*

If I leave the house at 8 a.m. to drive the 10 miles to work at an average of 10 miles per hour, what time do I arrive? *9 a.m*

It was 13°C two days ago. Yesterday the temperature rose 6°C. Today it dropped by 3°C. What is today's temperature? *16°C*

Complete the following:
2 + 3 − 1 = ?   99 x 2 = ?   30 + 45 = ?   *4*   *188*   *95*

True or false? If I'm 2 inches taller than Dave, and Dave is 5 inches shorter than Sam, then Sam is 3 inches taller than me. *True*

Which letter comes next in this pattern?
A B A C A D A ? *E*

Complete the following:
30 ÷ 10 = ?   50 ÷ 5 = ?   25 x 3 = ?   *3*   *10*   *75*

If I turn a combination lock 5 turns right, 3 turns left, 22 turns right, and then 4 turns left, how many turns from its starting position does the lock end up? *20 right*

Which of these words is a palindrome? (A palindrome reads the same both forwards and backwards.)
Moo   (Toot)   Food   Tool

If a windmill turns 5 revolutions per hour on a normal day, but twice as many revolutions per hour on a windy day, how many revolutions will it turn in 2 hours on a windy day?

20

Which of these words is the odd one out, and why?
Train   Coach   Truck   Bus   Taxi
Truck—it is the only one that isn't public transport.

Which number comes next in this sequence?
2   4   8   16   ?
32. The number doubles each time.

Airplane is to pilot as car is to?
Driver.

Which of these numbers gives the answer 9 if you add up all its individual digits?
123   456   135   247
135 (1 + 3 + 5 = 9).

How many hours are there in a weekend?
48 hours.

If I leave the house at 8 a.m. to drive the 10 miles to work at an average of 10 miles per hour, what time do I arrive?
9 a.m.

It was 13°C two days ago. Yesterday the temperature rose 6°C. Today it dropped by 3°C. What is today's temperature?
16°C.

Complete the following:
2 + 3 − 1 = ?   99 x 2 = ?   30 + 45 = ?
2 + 3 − 1 = 4   99 x 2 = 198   30 + 45 = 75

True or false? If I'm 2 inches taller than Dave, and Dave is 5 inches shorter than Sam, then Sam is 3 inches taller than me.
True.

Which letter comes next in this pattern?
A B A C A D A ?
E.

Complete the following:
30 ÷ 10 = ?   50 ÷ 5 = ?   25 x 3 = ?
30 ÷ 10 = 3   50 ÷ 5 = 10   25 x 3 = 75

If I turn a combination lock 5 turns right, 3 turns left, 22 turns right, and then 4 turns left, how many turns from its starting position does the lock end up?
20 turns (5 − 3 + 22 − 4).

Which of these words is a palindrome? (A palindrome reads the same both forwards and backwards.)
Moo   Toot   Food   Tool
Toot.

If a windmill turns 5 revolutions per hour on a normal day, but twice as many revolutions per hour on a windy day, how may revolutions will it turn in 2 hours on a windy day?
20 revolutions.

Memory Test

This time try and memorize where these vegetables occur in the grid. Then on the next page, you'll need to dig them up again and put them back in the same boxes. Spend a few minutes trying to memorize them.

Horseradish	Maris Piper Potato	Cucumber	Asparagus
Endive	Estima Potato	Radish	Carrot
Leek	Parsnip	Spinach	Cauliflower
Pea	Lettuce	Broccoli	Corn on the cob

Now see if you can recall where the vegetables were:

H	M		
E	E		C
L			C
P			C

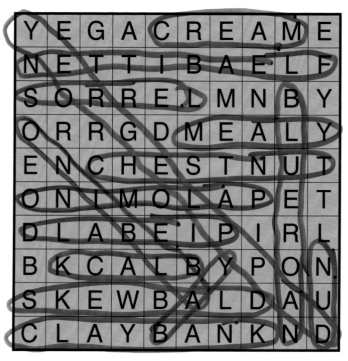

Try and find these colors of horse within the grid.

ALBINO

BAY

BLACK

BLUEROAN

CHESTNUT

CLAYBANK

CREAM

DAPPLEGREY

DUN

FLEABITTEN

MEALY

PALOMINO

PIEBALD

SKEWBALD

SORREL

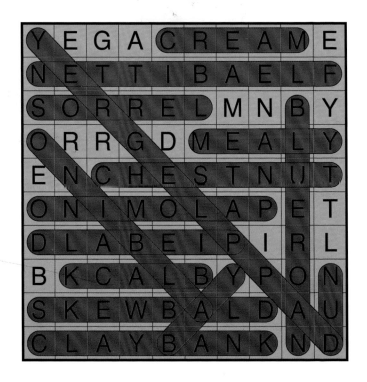

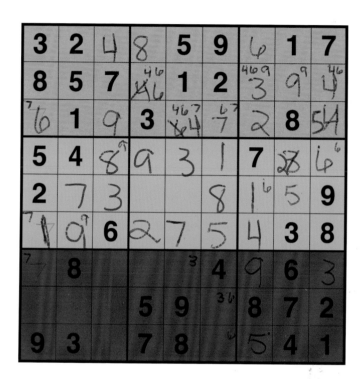

Sudoku

Sudoku has one very simple rule: fill in the grid so that each row, column, and marked 3 by 3 box contains each of the numbers 1 to 9 once and once only.

No guessing is required, and there is only one solution. If you're not sure you understand the rules, then take a quick peek at the answer to see how it works.

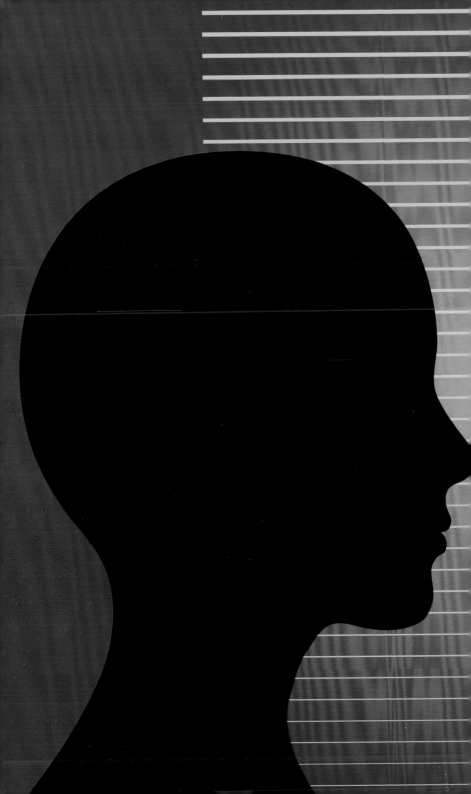

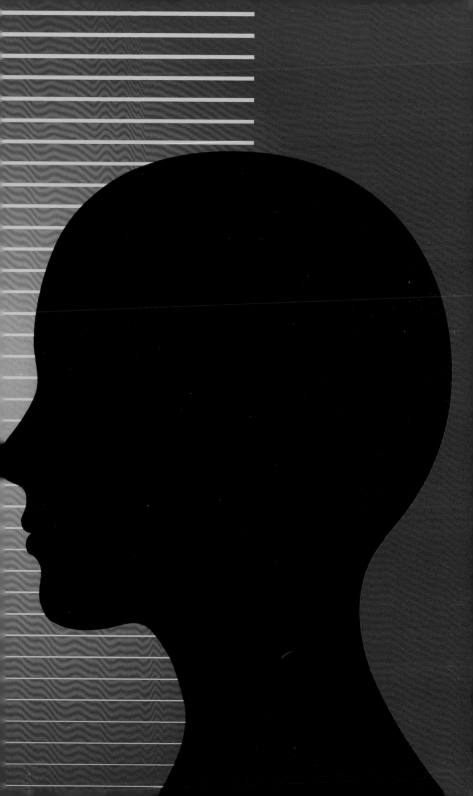

3	2	4	8	5	9	6	1	7
8	5	7	6	1	2	3	9	4
6	1	9	3	4	7	2	8	5
5	4	8	9	3	1	7	2	6
2	7	3	4	6	8	1	5	9
1	9	6	2	7	5	4	3	8
7	8	5	1	2	4	9	6	3
4	6	1	5	9	3	8	7	2
9	3	2	7	8	6	5	4	1

Which of these words is the odd one out, and why?
Green   Blue   Red   Orange   (Black)

Which number comes next in this sequence?
11   22   33   44   ?   *55*

Intelligent is to unintelligent as open is to?   *Closed*

If I write the number 35,478,353 with its digits in reverse order, which of these do I end up with?
35,387,435   35,347,835   35,353,874   (35,387,453)

Convert these to military time:
1:23 p.m.   5:30 a.m.   Midnight   8:30 p.m.   10 a.m.
13:23   05:30   24:00   20:30

My friend Simon goes running every day along a 6-mile circuit. It usually takes him an hour to make the circuit, so at what speed does he normally run?

If it's 17°C in London but 12°C in Edinburgh, how much hotter than Edinburgh is London?

Complete the following:
99 + 99 = ?   99 − 97 = ?   99 ÷ 99 = ?

True or false? If London Zoo has 5 monkeys, and Windsor Safari Park has 3 monkeys, then in total there are a maximum of 8 monkeys.

Which letter comes next in this pattern?
A B A B C A B C D A ?

Complete the following:
1 + 2 + 3 = ?   40 + 51 = ?   90 + 55 = ?

If I need 2 keys to open my front door but only 1 to open my back door, how many key turns do I make in total while fully unlocking and then fully locking both doors, assuming both doors were fully locked to start with and all keys require two turns to open or close a lock?

How many of these words have only one vowel?
Monkey   Chimp   Ape   Pie   Trip

If I paint 2 sheds green, 3 sheds blue, and 4 sheds yellow, and I use 2 cans of paint per shed, how many cans of paint do I need in total?

Which of these words is the odd one out, and why?
Green   Blue   Red   Orange   Black
Black—only one not a color of the rainbow.

Which number comes next in this sequence?
11   22   33   44   ?
55. Each number goes up by 11.

Intelligent is to unintelligent as open is to?
Closed.

If I write the number 35,478,353 with its digits in reverse order, which of these do I end up with?
35,387,435   35,347,835   35,353,874   35,387,453
35,387,453.

Convert these to military time:
1:23 p.m.	5:30 a.m.	Midnight	8:30 p.m.	10 a.m.
13:23	**05:30**	**00:00**	**20:30**	**10:00**

My friend Simon goes running every day along a 6-mile circuit. It usually takes him an hour to make the circuit, so at what speed does he normally run?
6 miles per hour.

If it's 17°C in London but 12°C in Edinburgh, how much hotter than Edinburgh is London?
5°C hotter.

Complete the following:
99 + 99 = ?   99 – 97 = ?   99 ÷ 99 = ?
99 + 99 = 198   **99 – 97 = 2**   **99 ÷ 99 = 1**

True or false? If London Zoo has 5 monkeys, and Windsor Safari Park has 3 monkeys, then in total there are a maximum of 8 monkeys.
True.

Which letter comes next in this pattern?
A B A B C A B C D A ?
B.

Complete the following:
1 + 2 + 3 = ?   40 + 51 = ?   90 + 55 = ?
1 + 2 + 3 = 6   **40 + 51 = 91**   **90 + 55 = 145**

If I need 2 keys to open my front door but only 1 to open my back door, how many key turns do I make in total while fully unlocking and then fully locking both doors, assuming both doors were fully locked to start with and all keys require two turns to open or close a lock?
12 turns.

How many of these words have only one vowel?
Monkey   Chimp   Ape   Pie   Trip
Two. Chimp and Trip.

If I paint 2 sheds green, 3 sheds blue, and 4 sheds yellow, and I use 2 cans of paint per shed, how many cans of paint do I need in total?
18 cans.

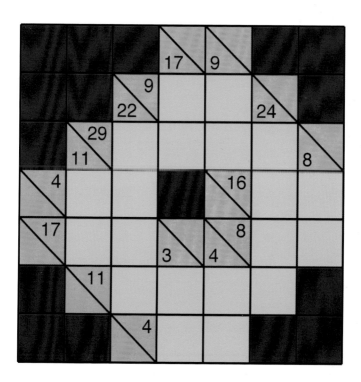

Kakuro

Fill in the grid so that each run of squares adds up to the total in the box above or to the left. You can only use the numbers 1 to 9, and you may not repeat any number within any run (a number may reoccur in the same row/column in a separate run). Totals below the diagonal line give the sum of the numbers in the run below, while totals to the right of the diagonal line give the sum of numbers in the run to the right.

No guessing is required, and there is only one solution. If you're not sure you understand the rules, then take a quick peek at the answer to see how it works.

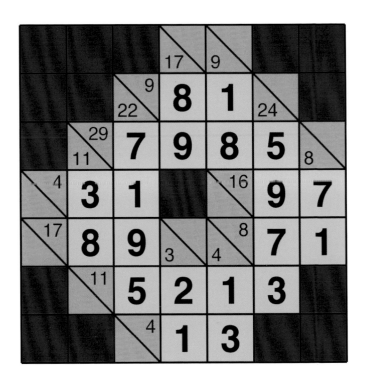

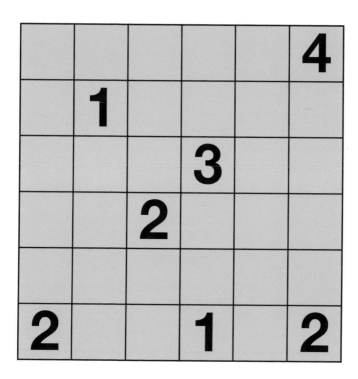

Nurikabe

Shade in squares in the grid in order to leave each number in a continuous unshaded area of the stated number of squares, bounded by shaded squares. Unshaded areas cannot touch in either a horizontal or vertical direction. All shaded squares must form a single continuous area, and there must be no 2x2 blocks of shaded squares.

No guessing is required, and there is only one solution. If you're not sure you understand the rules, then take a quick peek at the answer to see how it works.

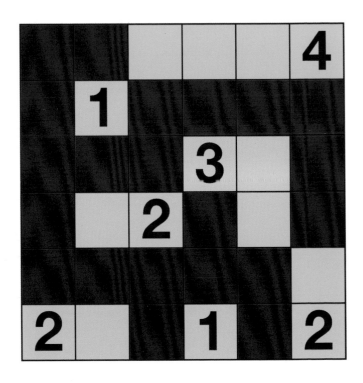

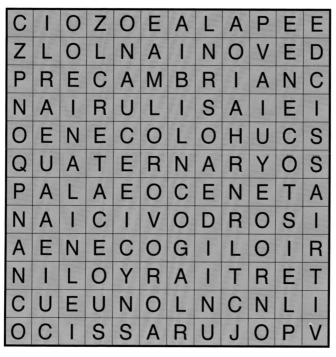

C	I	O	Z	O	E	A	L	A	P	E	E
Z	L	O	L	N	A	I	N	O	V	E	D
P	R	E	C	A	M	B	R	I	A	N	C
N	A	I	R	U	L	I	S	A	I	E	I
O	E	N	E	C	O	L	O	H	U	C	S
Q	U	A	T	E	R	N	A	R	Y	O	S
P	A	L	A	E	O	C	E	N	E	T	A
N	A	I	C	I	V	O	D	R	O	S	I
A	E	N	E	C	O	G	I	L	O	I	R
N	I	L	O	Y	R	A	I	T	R	E	T
C	U	E	U	N	O	L	N	C	N	L	I
O	C	I	S	S	A	R	U	J	O	P	V

See if you can find these geological terms hidden within the grid.

CRETACEOUS

DEVONIAN

HOLOCENE

JURASSIC

OLIGOCENE

ORDOVICIAN

PALAEOCENE

PALAEOZOIC

PLEISTOCENE

PRECAMBRIAN

QUATERNARY

SILURIAN

TERTIARY

TRIASSIC

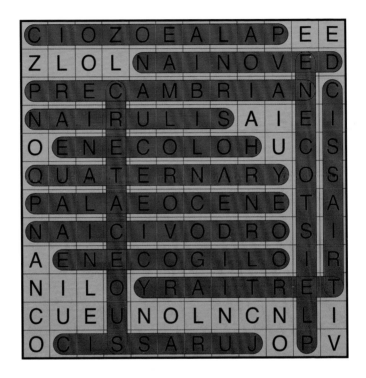

C	I	O	Z	O	E	A	L	A	P	E	E
Z	L	O	L	N	A	I	N	O	V	E	D
P	R	E	C	A	M	B	R	I	A	N	C
N	A	I	R	U	L	I	S	A	I	E	I
O	E	N	E	C	O	L	O	H	U	C	S
Q	U	A	T	E	R	N	A	R	Y	O	S
P	A	L	A	E	O	C	E	N	E	T	A
N	A	I	C	I	V	O	D	R	O	S	I
A	E	N	E	C	O	G	I	L	O	I	R
N	I	L	O	Y	R	A	I	T	R	E	T
C	U	E	U	N	O	L	N	C	N	L	I
O	C	I	S	S	A	R	U	J	O	P	V

Memory Test

I've placed 16 biscuits into boxes. See if you can remember where they are and then put them back in the same boxes on the next page. (Don't forget to put the lids on, or else they'll go stale . . .)

Flapjack	Digestive	Pretzel	Shortcake
Cracker	Bourbon	Matzo	Macaroon
Garibaldi	Wafer	Crispbread	Jaffa cake
Ginger nut	Rich tea	Shortbread	Oatcake

Now try and put the biscuits back in the same locations:

Flapjack			
	Bourbon		
		Crispbread	
			Oatcake

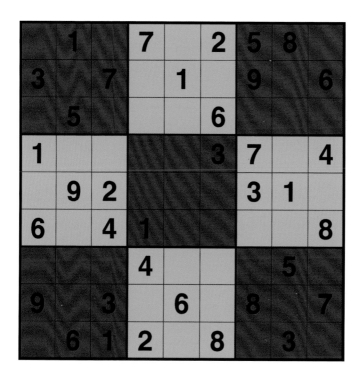

Sudoku

Sudoku has one very simple rule: fill in the grid so that each row, column, and marked 3 by 3 box contains each of the numbers 1 to 9 once and once only.

No guessing is required, and there is only one solution. If you're not sure you understand the rules, then take a quick peek at the answer to see how it works.

4	1	6	7	9	2	5	8	3
3	2	7	8	1	5	9	4	6
8	5	9	3	4	6	1	7	2
1	8	5	9	2	3	7	6	4
7	9	2	6	8	4	3	1	5
6	3	4	1	5	7	2	9	8
2	7	8	4	3	9	6	5	1
9	4	3	5	6	1	8	2	7
5	6	1	2	7	8	4	3	9

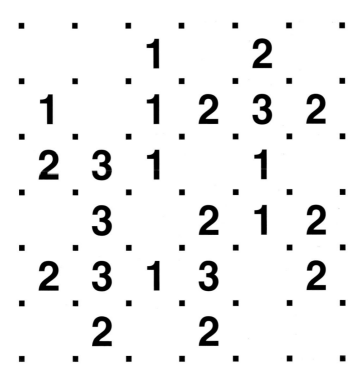

Slitherlink

Draw a single loop by connecting together the dots such that each numbered square has the specified number of adjacent line segments. You may only join dots by using straight horizontal or vertical lines, and the loop cannot cross or overlap itself in any way.

No guessing is required, and there is only one solution. If you're not sure you understand the rules, then take a quick peek at the answer to see how it works.

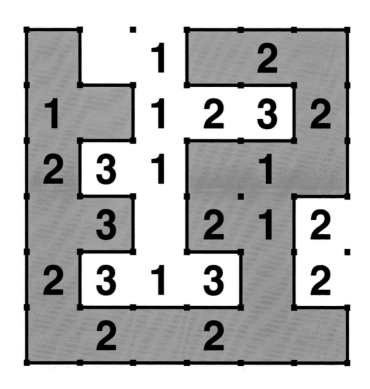

A	U	S	T	R	A	L	O	R	P	N	V
E	L	L	O	R	E	V	A	F	L	E	G
T	E	A	R	D	O	R	N	G	Y	W	E
T	G	X	P	O	A	H	D	T	M	H	G
O	H	E	I	R	A	G	A	W	O	A	B
D	O	S	N	K	H	R	L	M	U	M	A
N	R	S	G	I	A	U	U	I	T	P	N
A	N	U	T	N	P	B	S	N	H	S	T
Y	M	S	O	G	N	M	I	O	R	H	A
W	S	C	N	A	I	A	A	R	O	I	M
N	N	A	D	U	O	H	N	C	C	R	O
A	A	S	U	M	A	T	R	A	K	E	E

These are all types of chicken, just in case you didn't already know.
See if you can find them within the grid.

ANCONA	FAVEROLLE	ORPINGTON
ANDALUSIAN	HAMBURG	PLYMOUTH ROCK
AUSTRALORP	HOUDAN	SUMATRA
BANTAM	LEGHORN	SUSSEX
CAMPINE	MINORCA	WYANDOTTE
DORKING	NEW HAMPSHIRE	

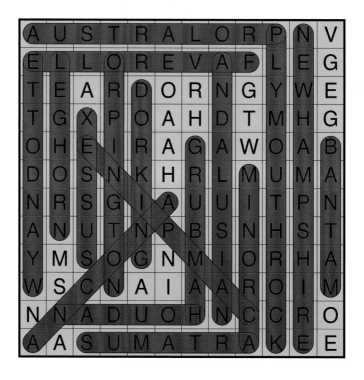

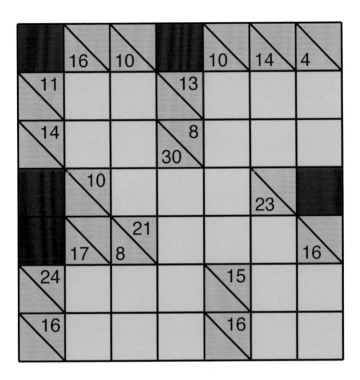

Kakuro

Fill in the grid so that each run of squares adds up to the total in the box above or to the left. You can only use the numbers 1 to 9, and you may not repeat any number within any run (a number may reoccur in the same row/column in a separate run). Totals below the diagonal line give the sum of the numbers in the run below, while totals to the right of the diagonal line give the sum of numbers in the run to the right.

No guessing is required, and there is only one solution. If you're not sure you understand the rules, then take a quick peek at the answer to see how it works.

	16	10		10	14	4
11	7	4	13	1	9	3
14	9	5	8 / 30	2	5	1
	10	1	6	3	23	
	17	21 / 8	9	4	8	16
24	9	7	8	15	6	9
16	8	1	7	16	9	7

Which of these words is the odd one out, and why?
Argentina   Austria   Ecuador   Mexico   Canada

Which number comes next in this sequence?
1   22   333   4444   ?

Live is to Evil as Dog is to?

Which of these numbers would look the same if viewed upside down?
99   66   696   888

If I'm 40 minutes late for an appointment and arrive at 3:30 p.m., what time should I have been there?

On weekdays I leave the house at 8 a.m. for a 20-minute journey into town. On Saturday I make the same journey, but leave two and a half hours later. What time do I arrive in town?

Today It's 70°F, but it's forecast to rise by 11°F during the day and then fall 18°F overnight. What temperature is it forecast to be overnight?

Complete the following:
10 x 10 = ?   100 x 100 = ?   5 x 50 = ?

True or false? If I start off with $100 and give away 25% to charity, I am left with only $25.

Which letter comes next in this sequence?
A E I O ?

Complete the following:
5 + 5 = ?   5 + 55 = ?   5 + 555 = ?

If I press the button "4" on my mobile phone I select G, then H, then I. How many times do I need to press "4" to type "GIG"?

Which of these word pairs are not homophones? (Homophones are words that sound the same but are spelled differently.)
Steak & Stake   Mousse & Moose   Mouse & Mice

If a week only had one day in it, how many weeks would there be in a 365-day year?

Which of these words is the odd one out, and why?
Argentina   Austria   Ecuador   Mexico   Canada
Austria—only one that isn't on the continent of America.

Which number comes next in this sequence?
1   22   333   4444   ?
55555.

Live is to Evil as Dog is to?
God. (Reverse the letters.)

Which of these numbers would look the same if viewed upside down?
99   66   696   888
888.

If I'm 40 minutes late for an appointment and arrive at 3:30 p.m., what time should I have been there?
2:50 p.m.

On weekdays I leave the house at 8 a.m. for a 20-minute journey into town. On Saturday I make the same journey, but leave two and a half hours later. What time do I arrive in town?
10:50 a.m.

Today it's 70°F, but it's forecast to rise by 11°F during the day and then fall 18°F overnight. What temperature is it forecast to be overnight?
63°F.

Complete the following:
10 x 10 = ?   100 x 100 = ?   5 x 50 = ?
10 x 10 = 100   100 x 100 = 10000   5 x 50 = 250

True or false? If I start off with $100 and give away 25% to charity, I am left with only $25.
False. I now have $75 left.

Which letter comes next in this sequence?
A E I O ?
U. Vowels.

Complete the following:
5 + 5 = ?   5 + 55 = ?   5 + 555 = ?
5 + 5 = 10   5 + 55 = 60   5 + 555 = 560

If I press the button "4" on my mobile phone I select G, then H, then I. How many times do I need to press "4" to type "GIG"?
5 times.

Which of these word pairs are not homophones? (Homophones are words that sound the same but are spelled differently.)
Steak & Stake   Mousse & Moose   Mouse & Mice
Mouse & Mice.

If a week only had one day in it, how many weeks would there be in a 365-day year?
365 weeks.

9			8	2	7			
1	7							4
	6	2						
7		3	6	4		9		
8				5				2
		6		9	8	1		7
						5	2	
4							9	6
			5	8	6			3

Sudoku
Sudoku has one very simple rule: fill in the grid so that each row, column, and marked 3 by 3 box contains each of the numbers 1 to 9 once and once only.
No guessing is required, and there is only one solution. If you're not sure you understand the rules, then take a quick peek at the answer to see how it works.

9	5	4	8	2	7	3	6	1
1	7	8	3	6	9	2	5	4
3	6	2	4	1	5	8	7	9
7	2	3	6	4	1	9	8	5
8	1	9	7	5	3	6	4	2
5	4	6	2	9	8	1	3	7
6	3	1	9	7	4	5	2	8
4	8	5	1	3	2	7	9	6
2	9	7	5	8	6	4	1	3

Read this recollection of a musical childhood and then answer as many questions as you can without checking the text again. Then when you've done that, go back and check the text and answer the rest.

I had my first tuneless experiments with the white notes at the age of six. Of course, being six and with grubby hands, all the notes ended up kind of off-white pretty quickly, but they were still better than the black notes. I didn't quite get those. They sounded funny, like when my sister tried to play her violin. I say tried, but really it was more trying for the rest of us than her, I think. Of course, now I'm on first name terms with the black notes. I quite like F sharp notes; B flats are another favorite. They show up sooner, you see; scales with less black notes. It's the way to go.

Trumpets. They're good too, although usually pretty loud; my sister didn't approve. I tried flutes, but I never could get my lips to work in the right way. My sister thought the silence was an improvement. I didn't much like my sister. Her trombone lessons were hardly quiet; she gave up right away. Big surprise.

Drums. You're less likely to play them out of tune, although you're less likely to play them at all—you don't need many drums in a school band. It's a shame. I had a natural flair for them. But this time even my parents didn't agree. They sided with my sister. No big surprise.

I wanted to learn the electric guitar, but I couldn't find anyone to give me lessons. And they said I should only learn four instruments at once; what did they know? I could have been a child prodigy, like a latter-day Chopin; except on the guitar. So I stuck to the piano; the black notes got friendlier; the white notes just got grubbier. Unfortunately, the piano tuning man said that it had gone a bit out of tune and it would always sound worse than my sister's cello (now she'd given up her other instruments), which was saying something. So I decided I'd just stick to the white notes; they're mostly in tune.

- What instrument did my lips seem incompatible with?
- Which two instruments did my sister play prior to the cello?
- What are my favorite "sharp" notes?
- What was the maximum number of instruments I was told I should learn at once?
- What did my sister think was too loud for me to play?
- How old was I when I first played the piano?
- What do I think was more trying for me than my sister?
- What did I have a natural flair for?
- Why couldn't I play the electric guitar?
- Why did I give up on black notes in the end?
- What put me off the drums?
- What sort of scales show up sooner, apparently?

What instrument did my lips seem incompatible with?
Flute.

Which two instruments did my sister play prior to the cello?
Violin and trombone.

What are my favorite "sharp" notes?
F sharps.

What was the maximum number of instruments I was told I should learn at once?
Four.

What did my sister think was too loud for me to play?
Trumpet.

How old was I when I first played the piano?
Six.

What do I think was more trying for me than my sister?
Her violin playing.

What did I have a natural flair for?
The drums.

Why couldn't I play the electric guitar?
I couldn't find anyone to give me lessons.

Why did I give up on black notes in the end?
They were out of tune.

What put me off the drums?
They weren't needed in the school band.

What sort of scales show up sooner, apparently?
Those with less black notes.

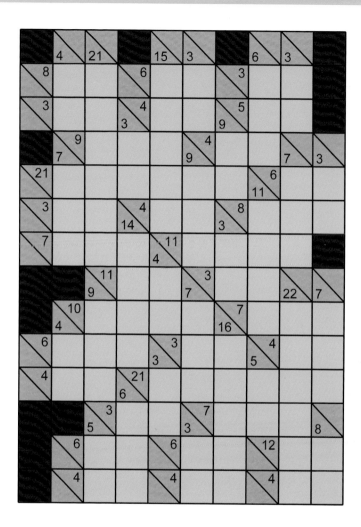

Kakuro

Fill in the grid so that each run of squares adds up to the total in the box above or to the left. You can only use the numbers 1 to 9, and you may not repeat any number within any run (a number may reoccur in the same row/column in a separate run). Totals below the diagonal line give the sum of the numbers in the run below, while totals to the right of the diagonal line give the sum of numbers in the run to the right.

No guessing is required, and there is only one solution. If you're not sure you understand the rules, then take a quick peek at the answer to see how it works.

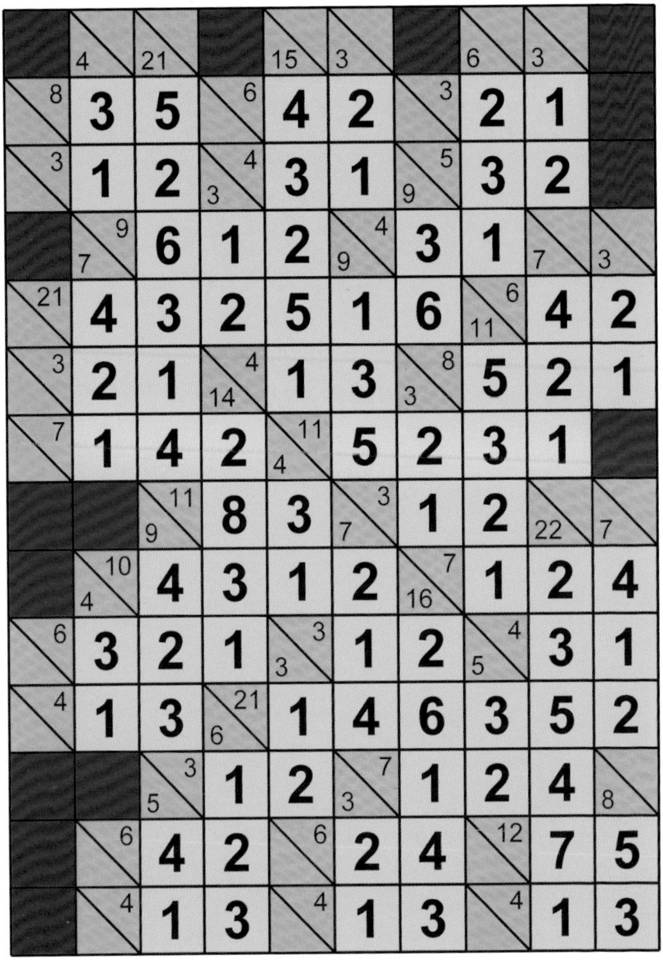

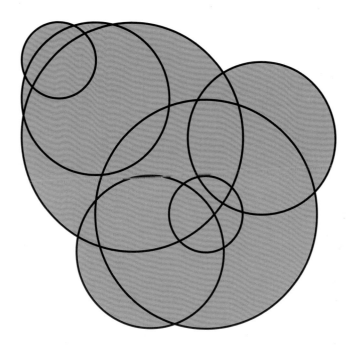

Try and answer these questions without marking on the paper (then mark on the paper and check your answers):

- How many circles can you count in this illustration?
- How many intersections are there where one circle crosses another?
- How many separate discrete areas are there in the picture?
- How many different sizes of circle are there?

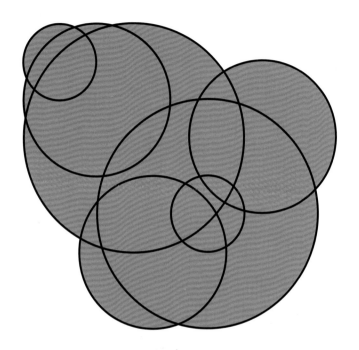

How many circles can you count in this illustration?
7 circles.

How many intersections are there where one circle crosses another?
24.

How many separate discrete areas are there in the picture?
25.

How many different sizes of circle are there?
3.

Which of these words is the odd one out, and why?
Monkey   Squirrel   Dog   Guinea pig   Cat

Which number comes next in this sequence?
1   2   3   5   8   ?

If I eat half a cake and then give a half of the remainder to my friend, how much of the cake is left?

If you write twenty-six million, four hundred thousand and twenty-six out in digits, which of these do you get?
26,400,026   264,026   26,426,000   260,420,026

How many seconds are there in an hour?

If I walk at 3 miles per hour for 50 minutes, how far have I traveled?

Given that water boils at 100°C and iodine boils at 184°C, how many degrees Celsius hotter do I need to heat iodine than water to boil it?

Complete the following:
26 + ? = 50   45 x ? = 90   ? + 33 = 66

If there are just three pairs of black and three pairs of white socks in a drawer, how many socks must I take out to be sure of getting one complete pair?

Which letter comes next in this pattern?
Z X Y W X V W ?

Complete the following:
25% of 100 = ?   15% of 100 = ?   75% of 80 = ?

If a section of fencing has fence posts every 1 meter, and the fence is 5 meters long, how many fence posts are there?

How many of these words have only one consonant?
Ape   Pie   Dog   Kid

If I use half a pint of milk to make pancakes on Tuesday, then buy another two pints of milk on Wednesday—of which I use a quarter to make several cups of tea—how much milk do I have left, given that I started with two and a half pints?

Which of these words is the odd one out, and why?
Monkey   Squirrel   Dog   Guinea pig   Cat
Guinea pig—only one without a visible tail.

Which number comes next in this sequence?
1   2   3   5   8   ?
13. Add the previous two numbers together.

If I eat half a cake and then give a half of the remainder to my friend, how much of the cake is left?
A quarter.

If you write twenty-six million, four hundred thousand and twenty-six out in digits, which of these do you get?
26,400,026   264,026   26,426,000   260,420,026
26,400,026.

How many seconds are there in an hour?
3600 seconds.

If I walk at 3 miles per hour for 50 minutes, how far have I traveled?
Two and a half miles.

Given that water boils at 100°C and iodine boils at 184°C, how many degrees Celsius hotter do I need to heat iodine than water to boil it?
84°C

Complete the following:
26 + ? = 50   45 x ? = 90   ? + 33 = 66
26 + 24 = 50   45 x 2 = 90   33 + 33 = 66

If there are just three pairs of black and three pairs of white socks in a drawer, how many socks must I take out to be sure of getting one complete pair?
4 socks. The first 3 could all be one color.

Which letter comes next in this pattern?
Z X Y W X V W ?
U.

Complete the following:
25% of 100 = ?   15% of 100 = ?   75% of 80 = ?
25% of 100 = 25   15% of 100 = 15   75% of 80 = 60

If a section of fencing has fence posts every 1 meter, and the fence is 5 meters long, how many fence posts are there?
6—don't forget you need one at the very start and the very end.

How many of these words have only one consonant?
Ape   Pie   Dog   Kid
Two. Ape and Pie.

If I use half a pint of milk to make pancakes on Tuesday, then buy another two pints of milk on Wednesday—of which I use a quarter to make several cups of tea—how much milk do I have left, given that I started with two and a half pints?
Three and a half pints.

Try and find these European languages hidden within the grid.

ALBANIAN	ERSE	LITHUANIAN
BASQUE	ESTONIAN	MALTESE
CASTILIAN	FAEROESE	MANX
CATALAN	FINNISH	NORWEGIAN
CORNISH	FRISIAN	PORTUGUESE
CROATIAN	GALICIAN	SARDINIAN
DANISH	GREEK	
ENGLISH	KARELIAN	

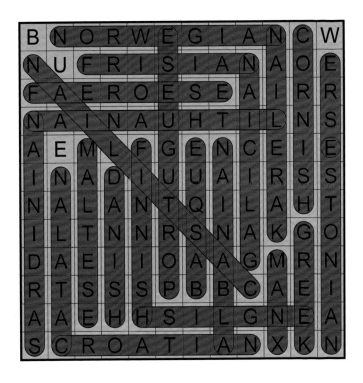

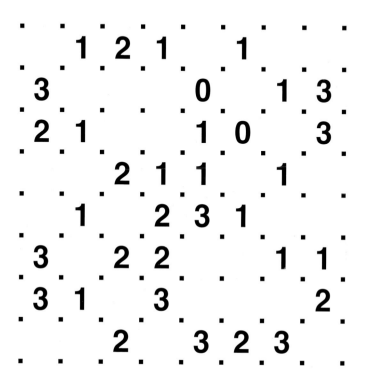

Slitherlink

Draw a single loop by connecting together the dots such that each numbered square has the specified number of adjacent line segments. You may only join dots by using straight horizontal or vertical lines, and the loop cannot cross or overlap itself in any way.

No guessing is required, and there is only one solution. If you're not sure you understand the rules, then take a quick peek at the answer to see how it works.

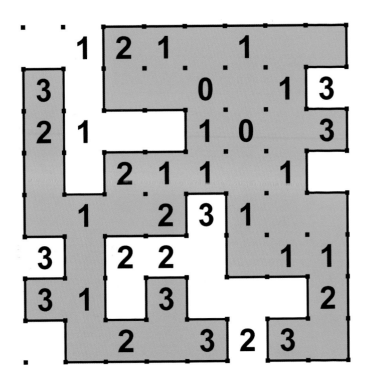

				7	1	3		
	7	3		4	6			
9			2				5	
3			8				1	
	1	5				7	9	
	2				5			3
	8				9			4
			1	6		9	2	
		4	7	8				

Sudoku

Sudoku has one very simple rule: fill in the grid so that each row, column, and marked 3 by 3 box contains each of the numbers 1 to 9 once and once only.

No guessing is required, and there is only one solution. If you're not sure you understand the rules, then take a quick peek at the answer to see how it works.

4	5	8	9	7	1	3	6	2
2	7	3	5	4	6	1	8	9
9	6	1	2	3	8	4	5	7
3	4	6	8	9	7	2	1	5
8	1	5	4	2	3	7	9	6
7	2	9	6	1	5	8	4	3
1	8	2	3	5	9	6	7	4
5	3	7	1	6	4	9	2	8
6	9	4	7	8	2	5	3	1

Memory Test

This grid has 25 rivers listed in it. See if you can remember which box they're in. You *don't* need to remember the names of the rivers themselves—just where they are. Take a few minutes to try and memorize them, then turn the page and place the list of rivers into the boxes.

Severn	Amazon	Nile	Dordogne	Niger
Isis	Jordan	Limpopo	Little Bighorn	Yukon
Volta	Thames	Tweed	Yangtze	Tay
Indus	Rio Grande	Moselle	Tyne	Churchill
Congo	Orinoco	Ouse	Cam	Barrow

Where did the rivers go?

Beware—there are a couple which weren't in the grid at all!

Moselle
Barrow
Tay
Isis
Severn
Little Bighorn
Tweed
Ouse
Nile
Clyde
Yukon
Cam
Churchill
Limpopo
Rio Grande
Orinoco
Thames
Rhone
Volta
Dordogne
Niger
Tyne
Jordan
Amazon
Indus
Congo
Yangtze

Kakuro

Fill in the grid so that each run of squares adds up to the total in the box above or to the left. You can only use the numbers 1 to 9, and you may not repeat any number within any run (a number may reoccur in the same row/column in a separate run). Totals below the diagonal line give the sum of the numbers in the run below, while totals to the right of the diagonal line give the sum of numbers in the run to the right.

No guessing is required, and there is only one solution. If you're not sure you understand the rules, then take a quick peek at the answer to see how it works.

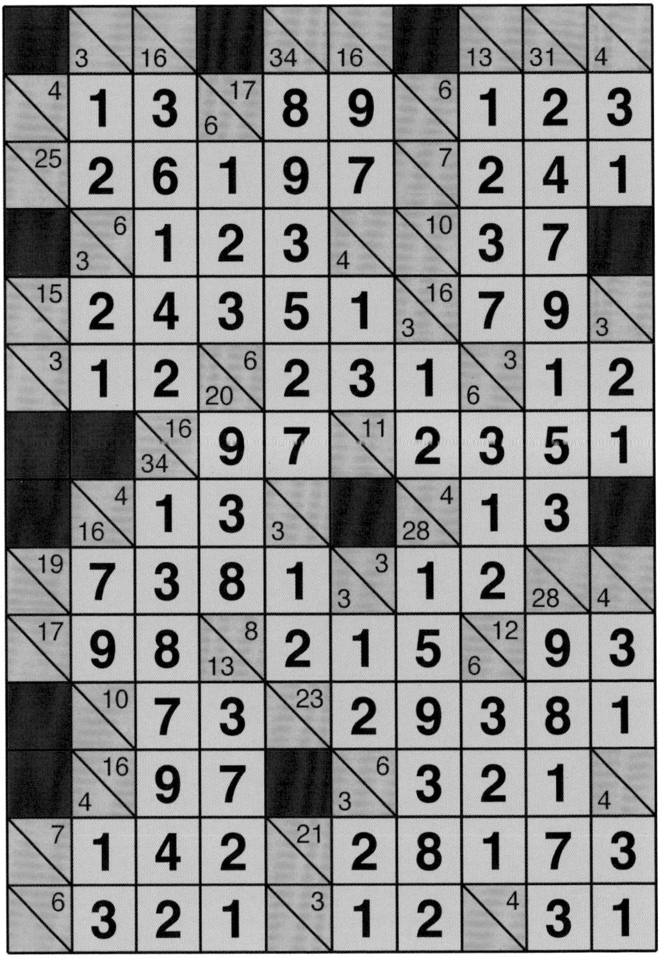

Which of these words is the odd one out, and why?
Echo   Lima   Bravo   Gin   Whiskey

Which number comes next in this sequence?
2   3   5   7   11   13   ?

If 50% of statistics are lies, but only 25% of lies are made by statisticians, how many lies are there in the average set of 100 statistics?

Think of a number. Add 15. Multiply by 2. Subtract 24. Subtract 2 times the number you thought of to start with. What number are you left with?

If I get up at 7:30 a.m. and spend an hour getting ready and traveling, then four hours working followed by an hour at lunch, what time will it be when I finish lunch?

If I drive at 60 mph and arrive home at 7 p.m., but leave work at 6:15 p.m., how many miles is my journey home?

To convert from Celsius to Kelvin, you add 273. If carbon boils at 3825°C, aluminium boils at 2792°K, and nickel boils at 3186°K, which boils at the highest temperature?

Complete the following:
33 + 66 = ?   99 x ? = 198   55 x 3 = ?

True or false? If all you know is that on Mondays I always go to the park after work, and on Tuesdays I always go to the zoo at lunchtime, this means that whenever I go to the park, it must always be Monday.

Which letter comes next in this pattern?
B C D G J O

Complete the following:
99% of 200 = ?   25% of 60 = ?   55% of 300 = ?

If the Sea of Tranquillity is on the Moon, and the Black Sea is on Earth, on which planet is the Red Sea?

How many of these words have only one consonant but two vowels?
Boo   Pie   Cat   Dog

If three-quarters of all supermarkets sell my favorite marmalade, and two-thirds of these don't have it in stock at the moment, what percentage of all supermarkets have my marmalade in stock?

Which of these words is the odd one out, and why?
Echo   Lima   Bravo   Gin   Whiskey
Gin—only one that isn't an alphabet communication code word.

Which number comes next in this sequence?
2   3   5   7   11   13   ?
17. They are all prime numbers (can only be divided a whole number of times by themselves and one).

If 50% of statistics are lies, but only 25% of lies are made by statisticians, how many lies are there in the average set of 100 statistics?
50 lies. The fact that 25% of lies are made by statisticians is irrelevant.

Think of a number. Add 15. Multiply by 2. Subtract 24. Subtract 2 times the number you thought of to start with. What number are you left with?
6.

If I get up at 7:30 a.m. and spend an hour getting ready and traveling, then four hours working followed by an hour at lunch, what time will it be when I finish lunch?
1:30 p.m.

If I drive at 60 mph and arrive home at 7 p.m., but leave work at 6:15 p.m., how many miles is my journey home?
45 miles.

To convert from Celsius to Kelvin, you add 273. If carbon boils at 3825°C, aluminium boils at 2792°K, and nickel boils at 3186°K, which boils at the highest temperature?
Carbon (at 4098°K).

Complete the following:
33 + 66 = ?   99 x ? = 198   55 x 3 = ?
33 + 66 = 99   99 x 2 = 198   55 x 3 = 165

True or false? If all you know is that on Mondays I always go to the park after work, and on Tuesdays I always go to the zoo at lunchtime, this means that whenever I go to the park, it must always be Monday.
False.

Which letter comes next in this pattern?
B C D G J O
P. Only curved capital letters are shown. (Or you might say T, since the letters are 1, 1, 3, 3, 5, 5, etc. apart.)

Complete the following:
99% of 200 = ?   25% of 60 = ?   55% of 300 = ?
99% of 200 = 198   25% of 60 = 15   55% of 300 = 165

If the Sea of Tranquillity is on the Moon, and the Black Sea is on Earth, on which planet is the Red Sea?
Also Earth.

How many of these words have only one consonant but two vowels?
Boo   Pie   Cat   Dog
Two. Boo and Pie.

If three-quarters of all supermarkets sell my favorite marmalade, and two-thirds of these don't have it in stock at the moment, what percentage of all supermarkets have my marmalade in stock?
25%.

N	A	E	B	O	C	A	J	P	R	B	R	B	N	Q
Z	A	L	F	O	O	N	Q	E	Y	O	G	A	E	R
C	L	I	A	A	R	H	G	Z	C	O	C	R	P	E
I	I	A	R	I	I	E	A	O	T	S	A	O	M	N
N	A	M	R	O	N	N	C	H	U	L	S	Q	U	A
O	E	U	N	C	T	O	I	T	U	T	V	U	D	I
I	N	N	Y	I	H	C	L	C	M	Z	A	E	E	S
T	R	A	N	S	I	T	I	O	N	A	L	U	J	S
A	V	E	R	C	A	D	D	V	C	H	Y	O	A	A
R	R	O	M	A	N	E	S	Q	U	E	D	N	R	N
E	U	Q	S	E	R	E	U	G	I	R	R	U	H	C
D	B	L	P	N	A	H	T	E	B	A	Z	I	L	E
E	S	R	I	M	S	I	L	A	T	U	R	B	U	S
F	E	S	O	C	L	A	S	S	I	C	A	L	M	C
P	T	S	I	C	I	S	S	A	L	C	O	E	N	Y

Try and find these architectural styles nestling within the grid.

BAROQUE

BRUTALISM

BYZANTINE

CHURRIGUERESQUE

CLASSICAL

COLONIAL

CORINTHIAN

ELIZABETHAN

FEDERATION

GOTHIC

IONIC

JACOBEAN

MUDEJAR

NEOCLASSICIST

NORMAN

PERPENDICULAR

POSTMODERNIST

REGENCY

RENAISSANCE

ROCOCO

ROMANESQUE

TRANSITIONAL

TUSCAN

VICTORIAN

				9	3	2		
		2	5		7	9	6	
						7	3	8
		2			3	5		
		1		9				
	6	3			5			
1	4	7						
	3	5	8		2	4		
		6	3	7				

Sudoku

Sudoku has one very simple rule: fill in the grid so that each row, column, and marked 3 by 3 box contains each of the numbers 1 to 9 once and once only.

No guessing is required, and there is only one solution. If you're not sure you understand the rules, then take a quick peek at the answer to see how it works.

7	8	4	6	9	3	2	1	5
3	1	2	5	8	7	9	6	4
6	5	9	4	2	1	7	3	8
4	9	1	2	6	8	3	5	7
5	7	8	1	3	9	6	4	2
2	6	3	7	4	5	1	8	9
1	4	7	9	5	6	8	2	3
9	3	5	8	1	2	4	7	6
8	2	6	3	7	4	5	9	1

See if your shopping trip would have been more successful than Doug's—read the following and then answer as many questions as you can without checking the text again. Then, when you've done that, go back and check the text and answer the rest.

Doug promised he'd do Sally's shopping this weekend. She knew it was a risk (Doug is pretty forgetful), but she was careful to tell him about the tube of teeth-whitening toothpaste he needed to buy, as well as all the standard groceries and other stuff. Two bags of oranges—they're "buy one get one free," so a bit of a bargain—and a bag of apples; but pick them by hand. Don't get the pre-packaged ones. Broccoli too; make sure it's loose—the wrapped-up florets are four times as expensive. It's crazy.

Not to mention the bread. Well okay, let's mention the bread. Not very exciting; pretty hard to get wrong, you'd have thought. And yet Doug did, three times. Quite a skill, Sally thought. Last week he'd got the thick stuff, not the thin, and the week before that it had been white, not brown—just not the same. And no French loaf at all; what was that all about? Apparently a ciabatta looked just as good. But it's not, is it? One's long and pointy; the other one, well, just isn't.

Three milks, each four pints, and two orange juices and an apple juice; one-liter cartons for those. Plus don't forget the newspaper on the way in—they didn't have any left at the corner store this morning—and if the coffee is still fifty percent off, then make sure you get two or three of those; no, make it four, I think. And tea. Can't go without tea. Get the little teabags with the strings to pull all the drips out; they're my favorite. They're in packs of eighty, so get two or three of them to last the month.

That should do. Oh yes—and some shampoo (not the green stuff; I didn't like that), some moisturizer (so long as it claims to be natural) and the spray deodorant I like with the letter H on the blue bottle. Not the purple. Although the green might do. One of those two, anyway. And then that's it. Well, except for the two C batteries and the forty-watt light bulbs.

Should be easy to remember that.

- What sort of broccoli shouldn't Doug buy, and why?
- What was Doug's mistake when buying bread two weeks ago?
- How many liters of juice in total does he have to buy?
- And if he forgot just one of the milks, how many pints would he buy?
- What did Doug find just as appealing as a French loaf?
- What letter identifies the deodorant Sally wants?
- And which other three toiletries does Sally ask Doug to buy?
- What sort of light bulb does Sally need?
- What's so good about the oranges at the moment?
- What sort of tea does Sally want?
- What does Doug need to remember on his way into the shop?
- What color of shampoo will Sally refuse to accept?
- How many batteries does Sally need?

What sort of broccoli shouldn't Doug buy, and why?
Wrapped-up florets—they cost four times as much.

What was Doug's mistake when buying bread two weeks ago?
He got white, not brown.

How many liters of juice in total does he have to buy?
Three.

And if he forgot just one of the milks, how many pints would he buy?
Eight pints.

What did Doug find just as appealing as a French loaf?
A ciabatta.

What letter identifies the deodorant Sally wants?
H.

And which other three toiletries does Sally ask Doug to buy?
Teeth-whitening toothpaste, natural moisturizer, and some shampoo.

What sort of light bulb does Sally need?
Forty-watt.

What's so good about the oranges at the moment?
They're "buy one get one free."

What sort of tea does Sally want?
Teabags with anti-drip strings to pull.

What does Doug need to remember on his way into the shop?
A newspaper.

What color of shampoo will Sally refuse to accept?
Green.

How many batteries does Sally need?
Two (C batteries).

```
2  2  3     3  2
      2     2     1  2
2  3  2        2     3
   2     2  1  0  1  2
3  3  2  3  2     3
2     2        2  2  2
3  3     2     2
      1  2     3  2  3
```

Slitherlink

Draw a single loop by connecting together the dots such that each numbered square has the specified number of adjacent line segments. You may only join dots by using straight horizontal or vertical lines, and the loop cannot cross or overlap itself in any way.

No guessing is required, and there is only one solution. If you're not sure you understand the rules, then take a quick peek at the answer to see how it works.

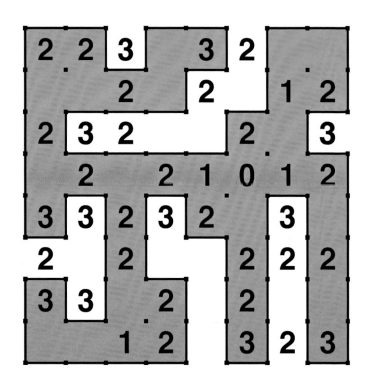

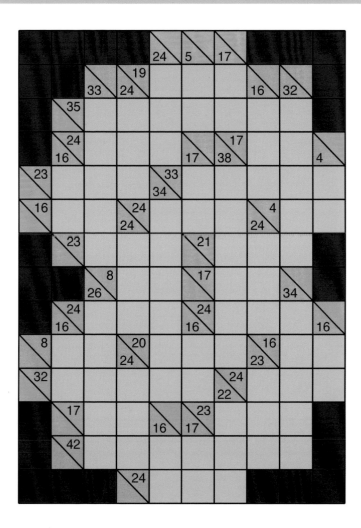

Kakuro

Fill in the grid so that each run of squares adds up to the total in the box above or to the left. You can only use the numbers 1 to 9, and you may not repeat any number within any run (a number may reoccur in the same row/column in a separate run). Totals below the diagonal line give the sum of the numbers in the run below, while totals to the right of the diagonal line give the sum of numbers in the run to the right.

No guessing is required, and there is only one solution. If you're not sure you understand the rules, then take a quick peek at the answer to see how it works.

			24\	5\	17\			
		33\	\19\24	7	3	9	16\	32\
	35\	3	7	9	2	8	1	5
	\24\16	7	9	8	17\	\17\38	8	9	4\
23\	9	6	8	\33\34	9	6	7	8	3
16\	7	9	\24\24	9	8	7	\4\24	3	1
	23\	8	9	6	\21	5	9	7
		\8\26	7	1	\17	9	8	34\
	\24\16	9	8	7	\24\16	8	7	9	16\
8\	7	1	\20\24	8	9	3	\16\23	7	9
32\	9	5	8	3	7	\24\22	9	8	7
	17\	8	9	16\	\23\17	9	8	6
	42\	3	7	9	8	5	6	4
			\24	7	9	8

Which of these words is the odd one out, and why?
Daffodil   Crocus   Iris   Daisy   Gladiolus

Which number comes next in this sequence?
12   14   13   15   14   ?

If I roll a die, I have a 1 in 6 chance of getting the number 1. If I roll two dice, what is the chance that I get a total of 2?

If politicians only tell the truth on Fridays, but they don't work Fridays in Congress, how much truth is spoken in Congress?

If I go to bed at 11:15 p.m. and get up at 7:30 a.m., how long have I been in bed?

I normally drive at an average of 30 mph, but today I need to slow to half my speed due to traffic. If my journey usually takes 20 minutes, how long does it take today?

To convert from Celsius to Fahrenheit, you multiply by 9 and then divide by 5, then add 32. If the temperature is 25°C, then what is it in Fahrenheit?

Complete the following:
26 x 3 = ?   99 x 3 = ?   45 + 145 = ?

True or false? The word "true" comes after "false" in the dictionary if you read it backwards, from the last page to the first page.

Which letter comes next in this sequence?
I V X L ?

Sort these into increasing order of value:
25% of $2   Half of $3   10 dimes

If humans are descended from apes, and apes are descended from amoebas, are humans descended from amoebas?

Which of these word pairs are not synonyms? (Synonyms are words which can have the same meaning.)
Rich & Wealthy   Happy & Sad   Far & Distant   Clear & Obvious

If a section of fencing has fence posts every 2 meters, and the fence is 56 meters long, how many fence posts are there?

Which of these words is the odd one out, and why?
Daffodil   Crocus   Iris   Daisy   Gladiolus
Daisy is the only flower that doesn't grow from a bulb.

Which number comes next in this sequence?
12   14   13   15   14   ?
16. The pattern is add 2, subtract 1, add 2, subtract 1, etc.

If I roll a die, I have a 1 in 6 chance of getting the number 1. If I roll two dice, what is the chance that I get a total of 2?
1 in 36. (You multiply 1 in 6 by 1 in 6 to get 1 in 36).

If politicians only tell the truth on Fridays, but they don't work Fridays in Congress, how much truth is spoken in Congress?
None.

If I go to bed at 11:15 p.m. and get up at 7:30 a.m., how long have I been in bed?
8 hours 15 minutes.

I normally drive at an average of 30 mph, but today I need to slow to half my speed due to traffic. If my journey usually takes 20 minutes, how long does it take today?
40 minutes. You don't need to know I normally drive at 30 mph.

To convert from Celsius to Fahrenheit, you multiply by 9 and then divide by 5, then add 32. If the temperature is 25°C, then what is it in Fahrenheit?
77°F.

Complete the following:
26 x 3 = ?   99 x 3 = ?   45 + 145 = ?
26 x 3 = 78   99 x 3 = 297   45 + 145 = 190

True or false? The word "true" comes after "false" in the dictionary if you read it backwards, from the last page to the first page.
False.

Which letter comes next in this sequence?
I V X L ?
C. They are Roman numerals in increasing order of value (I=1, V=5, X=10, L=50, C=100).

Sort these into increasing order of value:
25% of $2   Half of $3   10 dimes
25% of $2 (50 cents), 10 dimes (=$1), Half of $3 ($1.50)

If humans are descended from apes, and apes are descended from amoebas, are humans descended from amoebas?
Yes.

Which of these word pairs are not synonyms? (Synonyms are words which can have the same meaning.)
Rich & Wealthy   Happy & Sad   Far & Distant   Clear & Obvious
Happy & Sad.

If a section of fencing has fence posts every 2 meters, and the fence is 56 meters long, how many fence posts are there?
29, including the ones at both ends.

Memory Test

Here are 25 words arranged in a grid. This time you will need to remember not only the words, but also which box they're in. However, they're standard English words, so with the right memory techniques they should be easier to remember than the abstract lists of foods and rivers you've seen until now. Spend a few minutes trying to learn the following:

Dog	Leg	Monday	Park	Swing
Doll	Puddle	Weather	Night	Tuesday
Door	Television	Trampoline	Child	Zoo
Wednesday	Library	Shopping	Trainers	Party
Champagne	Key	Car	Bed	Thursday

Try and recall the words that were in the grid, and their positions:

Dog				

If you had difficulty, then you might find it easier to remember the words and their order if you try memorizing them as a story—e.g. "the **dog** bit my **leg** on **Monday**; I was in the **park** on the **swing**; a **doll** was in a **puddle** (puddle due to **weather**)" and so on. Why not go back and try again, if so?

G	S	C	R	O	Q	U	E	T	D	I	S	C	U	S
S	N	R	S	O	N	E	T	B	A	L	L	Y	B	G
H	S	I	L	C	U	R	L	I	N	G	L	A	C	N
A	O	C	E	V	O	L	L	E	Y	B	A	L	L	I
N	F	K	N	O	T	N	I	M	D	A	B	E	I	L
D	T	E	B	E	N	S	N	O	O	K	E	R	M	C
B	B	T	G	L	L	A	B	T	E	K	S	A	B	Y
A	A	U	V	N	S	S	C	G	E	G	A	B	I	C
L	L	A	B	T	O	O	F	S	N	N	B	R	N	A
L	L	W	I	N	D	S	U	R	F	I	N	G	G	R
L	A	C	R	O	S	S	E	L	N	T	N	I	U	C
I	S	R	E	D	N	U	O	R	K	A	A	N	S	H
J	A	V	E	L	I	N	H	O	C	K	E	Y	U	E
R	U	G	B	Y	H	S	A	U	Q	S	E	A	A	R
U	R	G	N	I	D	I	L	G	N	I	I	K	S	Y

Try and find these sports in the grid.

ARCHERY
BADMINTON
BASEBALL
BASKETBALL
CANOEING
CLIMBING
CRICKET
CROQUET
CURLING
CYCLING
DISCUS

FOOTBALL
GLIDING
GYMNASTICS
HANDBALL
HOCKEY
JAVELIN
LACROSSE
LUGE
NETBALL
RELAY
ROUNDERS

RUGBY
RUNNING
SKATING
SKIING
SNOOKER
SOFTBALL
SQUASH
TENNIS
VOLLEYBALL
WINDSURFING

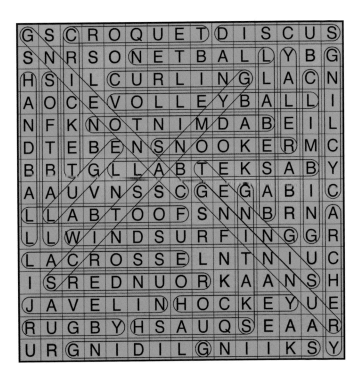

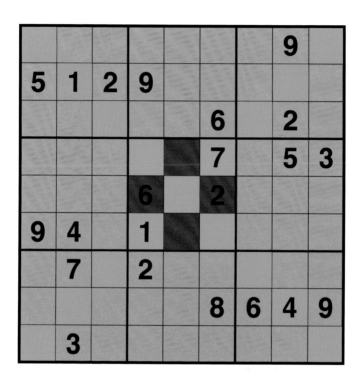

Sudoku X

Sudoku X is just as simple as standard Sudoku, except for the addition of a very simple extra rule: fill in the grid so that each row, column, diagonal, and marked 3 by 3 box contains each of the numbers 1 to 9 once and once only.

No guessing is required, and there is only one solution. If you're not sure you understand the rules, then take a quick peek at the answer to see how it works.

6	8	4	7	2	3	1	9	5
5	1	2	9	8	4	7	3	6
3	9	7	5	1	6	4	2	8
2	6	1	8	4	7	9	5	3
7	5	3	6	9	2	8	1	4
9	4	8	1	3	5	2	6	7
4	7	6	2	5	9	3	8	1
1	2	5	3	7	8	6	4	9
8	3	9	4	6	1	5	7	2

Which of these letters is the odd one out, and why?
C   O   H   X   N

Which number comes next in this sequence?
4   9   15   22   ?

If I throw three coins up in the air, what is the likelihood they all land showing heads?

If I can type a five-letter name in 5 seconds, and it takes me 6 seconds to type a six-letter name, but I can never find the "W" key and so it takes me three times as long to type "W" than any other letter, which name can I type faster—Wally or Andrew?

How many hours are there in a week?

It takes me 15 minutes to bicycle to work at an average speed of 10 miles per hour. If I bicycle to and from work each day, how many miles in total is my daily bicycle ride?

If Dave's sister marries Bob's brother, what relation is Bob to Dave?

Complete the following:
99 x 9 = ?   123 x 3 = ?   72 + 71 = ?

If Pete and Jane have 5 children, and each of their 5 children have 4 more children, and then half of those 4 children have 3 children of their own, but the other half only have 2 children, how many great-grandchildren do Pete and Jane have?

Which letter comes next in this sequence?
A B b c C D d e ?

If I weigh 80 kg and pick up a kilogram of heavy potatoes, while my friend weights 81 kg but picks up a kilogram of only light flowers, who now weighs the most in total?

If Tuesdays were only half the length of a normal day, how many complete weeks would there be in a year that started on a Monday, given that the year had 365 x 24 hours?

How many standard uppercase letters look the same when reflected in a mirror?

If bread and milk currently cost $2 to buy together, of which the bread accounts for 80 cents, how much will the milk cost if the price goes up by 10%?

Which of these letters is the odd one out, and why?
C   O   H   X   N
X—only letter that isn't a chemical element symbol.

Which number comes next in this sequence?
4   9   15   22   ?
30. The difference between the numbers increases by 1 each time.

If I throw three coins up in the air, what is the likelihood they all land showing heads?
1 in 8. (1 in 2 times 1 in 2 times 1 in 2).

If I can type a five-letter name in 5 seconds, and it takes me 6 seconds to type a six-letter name, but I can never find the "W" key and so it takes me three times as long to type "W" than any other letter, which name can I type faster—Wally or Andrew?
Wally—they both have one "w" in so this isn't relevant.

How many hours are there in a week?
168 hours.

It takes me 15 minutes to bicycle to work at an average speed of 10 miles per hour. If I bicycle to and from work each day, how many miles in total is my daily bicycle ride?
5 miles.

If Dave's sister marries Bob's brother, what relation is Bob to Dave?
Brother-in-law.

Complete the following:
99 x 9 = ?   123 x 3 = ?   72 + 71 = ?
99 x 9 = 891   123 x 3 = 369   72 + 71 = 143

If Pete and Jane have 5 children, and each of their 5 children have 4 more children, and then half of those 4 children have 3 children of their own but the other half only have 2 children, how many great-grandchildren to Pete and Jane have?
50 great-grandchildren. They have 20 grandchildren (5 x 4) of which half (10) have 2 children (10 x 2) and half have 3 children (10 x 3).

Which letter comes next in this sequence?
A B b c C D d e?
E. Alphabetical upper and lowercase sequences are interleaved two at a time.

If I weigh 80 kg and pick up a kilogram of heavy potatoes, while my friend weights 81 kg but picks up a kilogram of only light flowers, who now weighs the most in total?
My friend is still the heaviest.

If Tuesdays were only half the length of a normal day, how many complete weeks would there be in a year that started on a Monday, given that the year had 365 x 24 hours?
56 whole weeks. (In fact 393 days, since 365 x 24 = 8760 hours in a year, divided by (6 x 24 + 12) = 56 weeks and one day.)

How many standard uppercase letters look the same when reflected in a mirror?
11. A H I M O T U V W X Y. (You might count 10 if you draw your "Y"s at an angle.)

If bread and milk currently cost $2 to buy together, of which the bread accounts for 80 cents, how much will the milk cost if the price goes up by 10%?
$1.32.

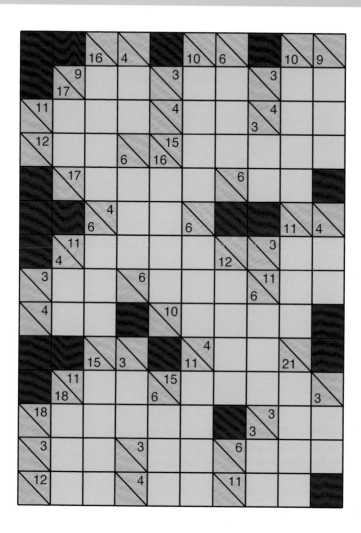

Kakuro

Fill in the grid so that each run of squares adds up to the total in the box above or to the left. You can only use the numbers 1 to 9, and you may not repeat any number within any run (a number may reoccur in the same row/column in a separate run). Totals below the diagonal line give the sum of the numbers in the run below, while totals to the right of the diagonal line give the sum of numbers in the run to the right.

No guessing is required, and there is only one solution. If you're not sure you understand the rules, then take a quick peek at the answer to see how it works.

		16	4		10	6		10	9
	17\9	6	3	\3	2	1	\3	2	1
11\	8	2	1	\4	1	3	3\4	1	3
12\	9	3	\6	15\16	4	2	1	3	5
	\17	5	2	7	3	\6	2	4	
	\6	4\	3	1	\6			11\	4
	4\11	3	1	5	2	12\	\3	2	1
3\	1	2	\6	3	1	2	6\11	8	3
4\	3	1		\10	3	4	2	1	
		15\	3		11\4	1	3	21\	
18\11	9	2	6\15	2	5	1	7	\3	
18\	7	2	1	3	5	3\3	2	1	
3\	2	1	\3	2	1	6\	1	3	2
12\	9	3	\4	1	3	11\	2	9	

6		3			2
					2
		1	3		
	2				2
	4				
		3	2		

Nurikabe

Shade in squares in the grid in order to leave each number in a continuous unshaded area of the stated number of squares, bounded by shaded squares. Unshaded areas cannot touch in either a horizontal or vertical direction. All shaded squares must form a single continuous area, and there must be no 2x2 blocks of shaded squares.

No guessing is required, and there is only one solution. If you're not sure you understand the rules, then take a quick peek at the answer to see how it works.

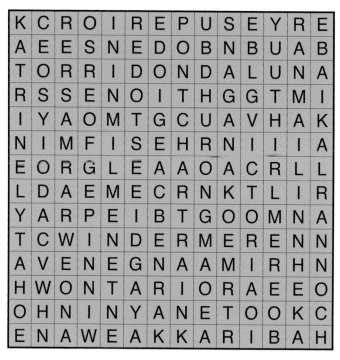

K	C	R	O	I	R	E	P	U	S	E	Y	R	E
A	E	E	S	N	E	D	O	B	N	B	U	A	B
T	O	R	R	I	D	O	N	D	A	L	U	N	A
R	S	S	E	N	O	I	T	H	G	G	T	M	I
I	Y	A	O	M	T	G	C	U	A	V	H	A	K
N	I	M	F	I	S	E	H	R	N	I	I	I	A
E	O	R	G	L	E	A	A	O	A	C	R	L	L
L	D	A	E	M	E	C	R	N	K	T	L	I	R
Y	A	R	P	E	I	B	T	G	O	O	M	N	A
T	C	W	I	N	D	E	R	M	E	R	E	N	N
A	V	E	N	E	G	N	A	A	M	I	R	H	N
H	W	O	N	T	A	R	I	O	R	A	E	E	O
O	H	N	I	N	Y	A	N	E	T	O	O	K	C
E	N	A	W	E	A	K	K	A	R	I	B	A	H

Try and find these lakes within the grid.

ANNECY	KARIBA	PONTCHARTRAIN
BAIKAL	KATRINE	RANNOCH
BELFAST	KOOTENAY	REINDEER
BODENSEE	LINNHE	SUPERIOR
ERIE	LOMOND	TAHOE
EYRE	MEAD	THIRLMERE
GENEVA	MEECH	TORRIDON
GRASMERE	NESS	VICTORIA
HURON	NICARAGUA	WINDERMERE
ILIAMNA	OKANAGAN	WINNIPEG
ILMEN	ONTARIO	

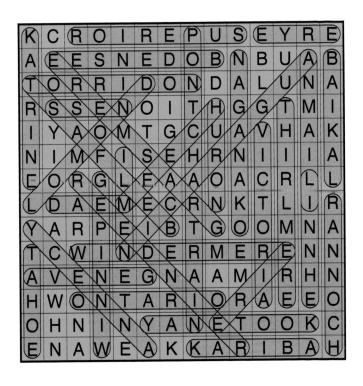

Memory Test

Try and remember these 25 vehicles and where they go in the grid. On the next page, each grid cell will contain the first letter of each vehicle that goes in it—the rest is up to you to remember!

Bicycle	Bus	Cab	Milk float	Taxi
Tanker	Tipper truck	Toboggan	Fire engine	Jet ski
Pram	Road-roller	Rickshaw	Aeroplane	Camper van
Coach	Train	Gritter	Scooter	Spacecraft
Tandem	Tank	Unicycle	Motorbike	Van

Now try and put the vehicles back where they were:

B	B	C	M	T
T	T	T	F	J
P	R	R	A	C
C	T	G	S	S
T	T	U	M	V

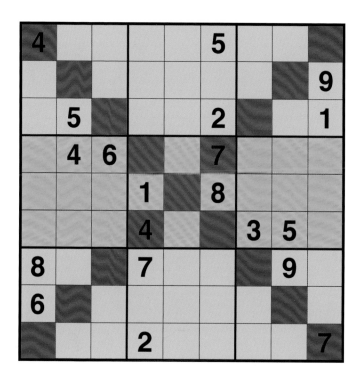

Sudoku X

Sudoku X is just as simple as standard Sudoku, except for the addition of a very simple extra rule: fill in the grid so that each row, column, diagonal, and marked 3 by 3 box contains each of the numbers 1 to 9 once and once only.

No guessing is required, and there is only one solution. If you're not sure you understand the rules, then take a quick peek at the answer to see how it works.

4	6	1	9	8	5	7	2	3
7	8	2	3	1	4	5	6	9
3	5	9	6	7	2	8	4	1
2	4	6	5	3	7	9	1	8
5	9	3	1	2	8	4	7	6
1	7	8	4	9	6	3	5	2
8	2	5	7	6	3	1	9	4
6	1	7	8	4	9	2	3	5
9	3	4	2	5	1	6	8	7

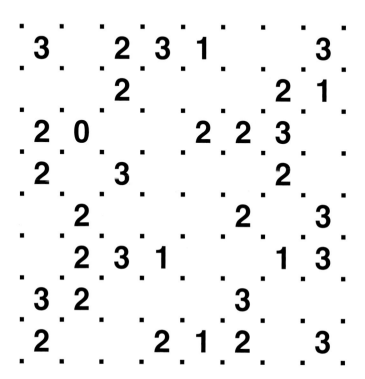

Slitherlink

Draw a single loop by connecting together the dots such that each numbered square has the specified number of adjacent line segments. You may only join dots by using straight horizontal or vertical lines, and the loop cannot cross or overlap itself in any way.

No guessing is required, and there is only one solution. If you're not sure you understand the rules, then take a quick peek at the answer to see how it works.

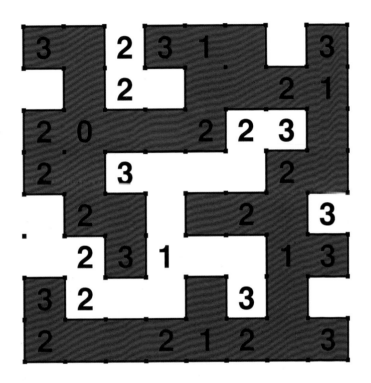

N	H	I	E	A	E	N	N	O	L	N	I	U	U	A	M	B	E
M	E	S	O	L	I	T	H	I	C	T	T	L	B	Y	N	E	I
N	A	I	R	E	T	S	U	O	M	I	N	M	C	N	C	C	E
R	A	G	V	I	O	I	E	O	S	L	D	E	A	I	I	I	B
S	I	O	D	A	I	N	I	G	O	O	N	A	E	E	A	I	N
A	B	E	N	A	I	L	I	Z	A	A	L	C	L	O	C	O	Y
C	I	H	T	I	L	O	E	N	E	E	S	U	N	L	E	U	I
G	H	O	T	C	M	E	N	A	V	M	Z	T	T	I	E	I	S
I	R	A	U	R	I	G	N	A	C	I	A	N	U	R	N	H	E
G	P	A	L	A	E	O	L	I	T	H	I	C	O	R	E	E	H
I	L	R	V	C	I	L	N	N	A	E	E	R	O	R	I	A	L
O	M	M	U	E	O	T	G	H	A	N	N	U	O	O	B	A	N
R	E	L	R	I	T	L	E	I	E	A	E	N	L	N	E	R	N
G	R	M	S	A	E	T	I	O	M	U	S	I	C	E	A	G	E
L	R	I	E	A	O	G	I	T	U	A	I	U	H	U	A	G	E
A	A	B	H	A	G	A	M	A	H	A	U	L	B	U	T	N	E
N	E	O	B	A	B	Y	L	O	N	I	A	N	T	N	P	N	N
O	A	N	E	A	N	G	H	E	I	L	C	H	B	G	T	T	N

See if you can find these archaeological periods or cultures hidden in the grid.

ACHEULEAN

ASTURIAN

AURIGNACIAN

AZILIAN

BRONZE AGE

CHALCOLITHIC

ENEOLITHIC

GRAVETTIAN

HELLADIC

ICEAGE

IRONAGE

LEVALLOISIAN

MAGDALENIAN

MESOLITHIC

MINOAN

MOUSTERIAN

MYCENAEAN

NEOBABYLONIAN

PALAEOLITHIC

SOLUTREAN

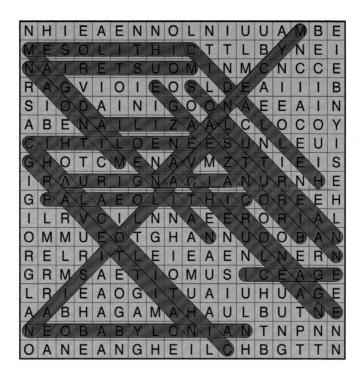

Kakuro

Fill in the grid so that each run of squares adds up to the total in the box above or to the left. You can only use the numbers 1 to 9, and you may not repeat any number within any run (a number may reoccur in the same row/column in a separate run). Totals below the diagonal line give the sum of the numbers in the run below, while totals to the right of the diagonal line give the sum of numbers in the run to the right.

No guessing is required, and there is only one solution. If you're not sure you understand the rules, then take a quick peek at the answer to see how it works.

A Kakuro grid puzzle solution. Clue cells and filled answer digits:

		13\	\3		17\	\11		10\	\11
	\4 3\	3	1	\4	1	3	\3	2	1
10\	1	7	2	\16 11\	9	7	\4 23\	1	3
\3	2	1	\21 6\	2	4	1	6	3	5
	\10	2	1	4	3	\15 17\	9	4	2
		\7 18\	2	5	\9 10\	1	8	15\	16\
	\12 16\	9	3	\16 23\	7	9	16\	7	9
14\	9	5	\16	8	1	7	\9 7\	2	7
11\	7	4	\8 24\	6	2	\8 24\	2	6	
	\29 22\	7	9	\11 11\	7	4	30\		
24\	9	7	8	\21 10\	5	9	1	6	16\
38\	7	5	9	6	3	8	\16 9\	7	9
6\	5	1	\3	1	2	17\	2	8	7
17\	8	9	\4	3	1	16\	7	9	

140

Which of these words is the odd one out, and why?
Mouse   Frog   Newt   Toad   Salamander

Which number comes next in this sequence?
1   2   2   4   8   32   ?

In what way are these word pairs related?
Retails & Saltier   Melon & Lemon

Which one of these words would still read as an English word when viewed in a mirror?
MOTTO   THAW   MOOD   TOMATO   OH

How many minutes are there in a day?

This evening I drive 10 miles from work, stop to do some shopping, then drive 15 miles home. Later on I drive 5 miles to a restaurant and then back. How far have I driven this evening?

To convert from Celsius to Fahrenheit, you multiply by 9 and then divide by 5, then add 32. If the temperature is 10°C, then what is it in Fahrenheit?

Complete the following:
55 + 45 + 35 = ?   99 + 89 + 79 = ?   61 + 49 − 53 = ?

How many different uppercase letters can be accurately represented on a standard 7-segment number display as you typically find on digital watches and clocks?

Which letter comes next in this pattern?
T W T F S ?

Complete the following:
987 + 123 = ?   55 x 4 = ?   26 x 4 = ?

If today is three days after Tuesday, and tomorrow will be five days before my birthday, what day is my birthday on?

If all vowels are replaced such that A becomes U, E becomes A, I becomes E, O becomes I, and U becomes O, what unlikely occurrence is being reported here?
Carry on dug perk.

If I buy some shares whose value then goes up by 10% to 88 cents per share, and I have 50 shares, what was the previous total value of my shares?

Which of these words is the odd one out, and why?

Mouse   Frog   Newt   Toad   Salamander

Mouse—only one that isn't an amphibian.

Which number comes next in this sequence?

1   2   2   4   8   32   ?

256. Each number is equal to the previous two numbers multiplied together.

In what way are these word pairs related?

Retails & Saltier   Melon & Lemon

The word pairs are anagrams of each other.

How many minutes are there in a day?

1440 minutes.

This evening I drive 10 miles from work, stop to do some shopping, then drive 15 miles home. Later on I drive 5 miles to a restaurant and then back. How far have I driven this evening?

35 miles.

To convert from Celsius to Fahrenheit, you multiply by 9 and then divide by 5, then add 32. If the temperature is 10°C, then what is it in Fahrenheit?

50°F.

Complete the following:

55 + 45 + 35 = ?   99 + 89 + 79 = ?   61 + 49 – 53 = ?

55 + 45 + 35 = 135   99 + 89 + 79 = 267   61 + 49 – 53 = 57

How many different uppercase letters can be accurately represented on a standard 7-segment number display as you typically find on digital watches and clocks?

13: A C E F G H I J L O P S U. (Or 14 if you include Y.)

Which letter comes next in this pattern?

T W T F S ?

S. They are the first letter of the days of the week starting from Tuesday.

Complete the following:

987 + 123 = ?   55 x 4 = ?   26 x 4 = ?

987 + 123 = 1110   55 x 4 = 220   26 x 4 = 104

If today is three days after Tuesday, and tomorrow will be five days before my birthday, what day is my birthday on?

Thursday.

If all vowels are replaced such that A becomes U, E becomes A, I becomes E, O becomes I, and U becomes O, what unlikely occurrence is being reported here?

Carry on dug perk.

Curry in dog park.

If I buy some shares whose value then goes up by 10% to 88 cents per share, and I have 50 shares, what was the previous total value of my shares?

$40.

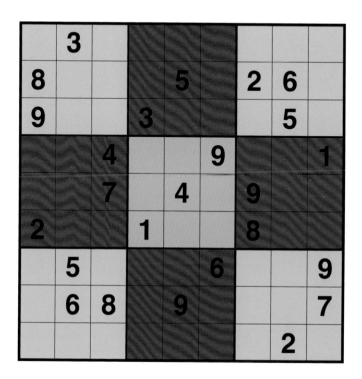

Sudoku

Sudoku has one very simple rule: fill in the grid so that each row, column, and marked 3 by 3 box contains each of the numbers 1 to 9 once and once only.

No guessing is required, and there is only one solution. If you're not sure you understand the rules, then take a quick peek at the answer to see how it works.

4	3	5	6	2	1	7	9	8
8	7	1	9	5	4	2	6	3
9	2	6	3	7	8	1	5	4
5	8	4	2	3	9	6	7	1
6	1	7	8	4	5	9	3	2
2	9	3	1	6	7	8	4	5
7	5	2	4	1	6	3	8	9
3	6	8	5	9	2	4	1	7
1	4	9	7	8	3	5	2	6

Here's the thrilling story of five continental campers. Read this passage and then answer as many questions as you can without checking the text again. Then when you've done that, go back and check the text and answer the rest.

Bob, Dave, George, Sue, and Caron decide to go camping in France. They pack themselves and everything they need into two cars and set off on the three-hour trip to the ferry, followed by the hour-long crossing and another four hours en route to the campsite. When they get to the campsite, it's dark, so it takes them another half an hour to find their spot. By the time they've set up their tents, another couple of hours have passed.

The next morning, they wake up to see that there are only seven other groups of people staying at the campsite, but that there are three streams within an easy walk of the site. Dave and Sue decide to go off to Le Brook while the other three head off to Le Canal and Le Big River (those are the names that they decide to call them, anyway). On the way, George buys some supplies using the fifty euros he has with him, getting just five euros sixty cents in change—not enough to buy more than two cups of coffee at current campsite rates! Last year the prices were a third less.

Over the next three days, they explore all five of the paths heading away from the site, with George and Caron taking over two hundred photos between them of the local flora and fauna. Bob thinks that's far too many photos; he's made do with a single roll of thirty-six.

Two days later their trip is over, so they set off on the journey back: all two hundred and thirteen miles back to the ferry crossing and then one hundred and sixty miles back from the other side. It's at least ten o'clock in the evening before they're home.

- How many hours did it take after they left the ferry before they had their tents fully set up?
- How many groups of people in total were now staying at the campsite?
- What names did the group give to the three streams in the area?
- How much money did George spend on supplies on the first morning?
- How much cheaper was campsite coffee the year before?
- Which couple took over two hundred photos?
- What time was it past when they all arrived home after the holiday?
- Why did it take them a while to find their spot on arrival?
- How many cars did they take to France?
- Who was in the group of two that went off to investigate a stream on the first day?
- How many paths led away from the campsite?
- How long did the trip to the ferry take from their homes?
- What was the total distance they drove home?

How many hours did it take after they left the ferry before they had their tents fully set up?
Six and a half hours.

How many groups of people in total were now staying at the campsite?
Eight, including the group in the story.

What names did the group give to the three streams in the area?
Le Brook, Le Canal, and Le Big River.

How much money did George spend on supplies on the first morning?
Forty-four euros and forty cents.

How much cheaper was campsite coffee the year before?
A third less.

Which couple took over two hundred photos?
George and Caron.

What time was it past when they all arrived home after the holiday?
Ten o'clock.

Why did it take them a while to find their spot on arrival?
It was dark.

How many cars did they take to France?
Two cars.

Who was in the group of two that went off to investigate a stream on the first day?
Dave and Sue.

How many paths led away from the campsite?
Five.

How long did the trip to the ferry take from their homes?
Three hours.

What was the total distance they drove home?
Three hundred and seventy-three miles.

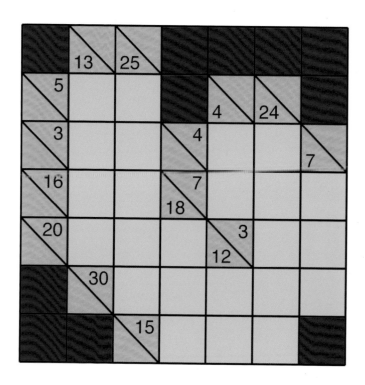

Kakuro

Fill in the grid so that each run of squares adds up to the total in the box above or to the left. You can only use the numbers 1 to 9, and you may not repeat any number within any run (a number may reoccur in the same row/column in a separate run). Totals below the diagonal line give the sum of the numbers in the run below, while totals to the right of the diagonal line give the sum of numbers in the run to the right.

No guessing is required, and there is only one solution. If you're not sure you understand the rules, then take a quick peek at the answer to see how it works.

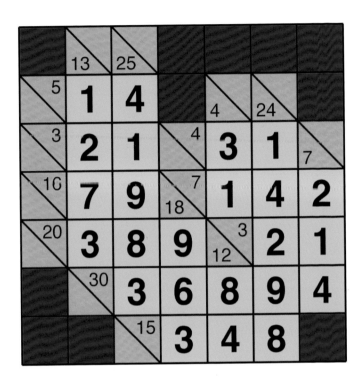

- How many triangles are there in this illustration?
- How many right-angled triangles are there? (◣)
- How many X's are formed at the line intersections in this illustration?
- How many rectangles are there?

How many triangles are there in this illustration?
There are at least 30.

How many right-angled triangles are there?
There are at least 13.

How many X's are formed at the line intersections in this illustration?
7.

How many rectangles are there?
There are at least 28.

Which of these words is the odd one out, and why?
Mile   Acre   Kilometer   Furlong

Which number comes next in this sequence?
7   8   9   4   5   6   ?

Right-wing is to left-wing as port is to?

Which of these numbers is divisible by 3 into a whole number?
123   302   959

How many minutes are there in twenty-three hours?

If one train leaves a station at 3:30 p.m. and travels at an average of 50 mph, and a second train leaves the same station at 3:45 p.m. but travels at an average of 60 mph, which will be first to arrive at a station 50 miles down the track?

Today is the hottest day of the year, and the coldest day was 20°C colder than this, but that cold day was still 7°C above the lowest ever recorded; today also happens to be the same margin below the hottest temperature recorded. If the hottest temperature ever recorded is 29°C, what is the lowest temperature ever recorded?

Complete the following:
13 x 12 = ?   46 x ? = 230   246 + 357 = ?

Our decimal number system of 0 to 9 followed by 10 to 19 and so on uses 10 different digits, 0–9. The binary number system works in the same way, but uses only two different digits, 0 and 1. This means that 0(decimal) = 0(binary), 1(decimal) = 1(binary), but 2(decimal) = 10(binary), 3(decimal) = 11(binary), 4(decimal) = 100(binary), and so on. Given this, convert the following numbers into binary:
5   7   8   15

Which letter comes next in this pattern?
A E F H I ?

Complete the following:
0.25 x 4 = ?   Half of 94 = ?   ½ x ½ = ?

If a horse has to jump 15 fences to complete a lap of a circuit, but completes only two-thirds of the course before pulling up short at a fence, given that the course consists of 2 laps, how many fences did the horse jump? Assume the fences are evenly spaced around the lap and that the first fence is not precisely on the start line.

Which of these place-denoting words or alternative spellings thereof is not an anagram of "retainer"?
Aretine Eritrean Arretine

What is the sum of all the numbers from 1 to 9?

Which of these words is the odd one out, and why?

Mile   Acre   Kilometer   Furlong

Kilometer—only one that is a metric measurement, not imperial.

Which number comes next in this sequence?

7   8   9   4   5   6   ?

1. They are the numbers on a keyboard number pad reading across from top to bottom and left to right.

Right-wing is to left-wing as port is to?

Starboard.

Which of these numbers is divisible by 3 into a whole number?

123   302   959

123.

How many minutes are there in twenty-three hours?

1380 minutes.

If one train leaves a station at 3:30 p.m. and travels at an average of 50 mph, and a second train leaves the same station at 3:45 p.m. but travels at an average of 60 mph, which will be first to arrive at a station 50 miles down the track?

The earlier train will arrive at 4:30 p.m.; the later train will arrive at 4:35 p.m. So the earlier train will arrive first.

Today is the hottest day of the year, and the coldest day was 20°C colder than this, but that cold day was still 7°C above the lowest ever recorded; today also happens to be the same margin below the hottest temperature recorded. If the hottest temperature ever recorded is 29°C, what is the lowest temperature ever recorded?

-5°C.

Complete the following:

13 x 12 = ?   46 x ? = 230   246 + 357 = ?

13 x 12 = 156   46 x 5 = 230   246 + 357 = 603

Our decimal number system of 0 to 9 followed by 10 to 19 and so on uses 10 different digits, 0–9. The binary number system works in the same way but uses only two different digits, 0 and 1. This means that 0(decimal) = 0(binary), 1(decimal) = 1(binary) but 2(decimal) = 10(binary), 3(decimal) = 11(binary), 4(decimal) = 100(binary), and so on. Given this, convert the following numbers into binary:

5   7   8   15

101   111   1000   1111

Which letter comes next in this pattern?

A E F H I ?

K. The sequence consists of uppercase letters without any curved parts.

Complete the following:

0.25 x 4 = ?   Half of 94 = ?   ½ x ½ = ?

0.25 x 4 = 1   Half of 94 = 47   ½ x ½ = ¼

If a horse has to jump 15 fences to complete a lap of a circuit, but completes only two-thirds of the course before pulling up short at a fence, given that the course consists of 2 laps, how many fences did the horse jump? Assume the fences are evenly spaced around the lap and that the first fence is not precisely on the start line.

19 fences.

Which of these place-denoting words or alternative spellings thereof is not an anagram of "retainer"?

Aretine   Eritrean   Arretine

Aretine.

What is the sum of all the numbers from 1 to 9?

45.

B	D	A	Y	T	T	E	R	B	I	U	M	C	R	H
E	L	E	A	D	P	A	L	L	A	D	I	U	M	M
R	L	M	A	Z	L	B	O	R	O	N	T	O	U	U
Y	A	G	I	I	A	O	B	O	E	H	L	N	I	I
L	N	E	T	R	U	G	S	E	Y	I	L	N	S
L	T	R	E	C	I	D	R	N	B	M	M	M	I	E
I	H	M	L	O	N	A	I	D	U	U	U	E	L	N
U	A	A	L	N	U	U	E	L	I	I	I	U	O	G
M	N	N	U	I	M	N	A	M	T	S	S	R	D	A
U	U	I	R	U	U	I	Y	N	L	S	O	O	A	M
I	M	U	I	M	Y	D	O	E	S	A	R	P	G	U
B	K	M	U	I	O	R	K	L	A	T	P	I	S	I
O	S	U	M	E	T	C	N	I	Z	O	S	U	I	M
I	R	O	N	S	I	L	V	E	R	P	Y	M	E	S
N	E	S	E	N	A	G	N	A	M	Y	D	M	M	O

These metals are all hidden within the grid—seek them out!

ALUMINUM	LANTHANUM	PLATINUM
ARSENIC	LEAD	POTASSIUM
BERYLLIUM	MAGNESIUM	PRASEODYMIUM
BORON	MANGANESE	RUTHENIUM
DYSPROSIUM	MOLYBDENUM	SILVER
EUROPIUM	NEODYMIUM	STRONTIUM
GADOLINIUM	NICKEL	TELLURIUM
GERMANIUM	NIOBIUM	YTTERBIUM
GOLD	OSMIUM	ZINC
IRON	PALLADIUM	ZIRCONIUM

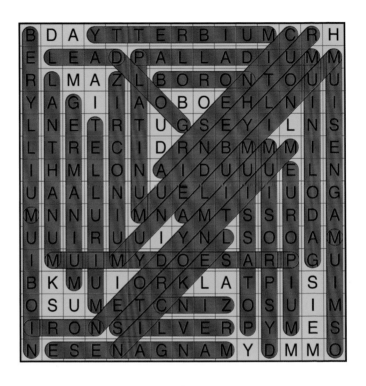

```
3      2 2 3    2 2
   2     2 0      1 2
 2      2 2     3     3 2
 2 0 3      2       1           2
         1       2 1 3      2
 2      3 2 3     1
 1        1     2     3 2 3
    3 2      2     2 2       2
       2 1     2 3       3
    2 3    2 2 3       2
```

Slitherlink

Draw a single loop by connecting together the dots such that each numbered square has the specified number of adjacent line segments. You may only join dots by using straight horizontal or vertical lines, and the loop cannot cross or overlap itself in any way.

No guessing is required, and there is only one solution. If you're not sure you understand the rules, then take a quick peek at the answer to see how it works.

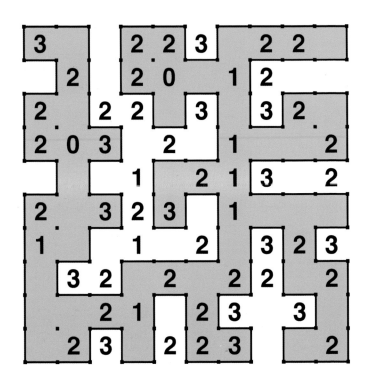

					8		3	4
				6	3		2	
				1	2		8	7
		5					4	
8								1
	7					9		
3	8		2	5				
	1		9	4				
7	4		8					

Sudoku
Sudoku has one very simple rule: fill in the grid so that each row, column, and marked 3 by 3 box contains each of the numbers 1 to 9 once and once only.
No guessing is required, and there is only one solution. If you're not sure you understand the rules, then take a quick peek at the answer to see how it works.

1	2	7	5	9	8	6	3	4
4	5	8	7	6	3	1	2	9
9	6	3	4	1	2	5	8	7
6	3	5	1	7	9	8	4	2
8	9	4	3	2	5	7	6	1
2	7	1	6	8	4	9	5	3
3	8	9	2	5	7	4	1	6
5	1	2	9	4	6	3	7	8
7	4	6	8	3	1	2	9	5

Memory Test

Here are 30 apparently random words—try and remember not only the words, but also where they go in the grid. There will be no clues in the grid on the following page.

Cell phone	Pen	Television	House	Door
Pen pal	Desk	Lost	Book	Memory
Friend	Silver birch	Fence post	Mailman	Tricycle
Trumpet	Golden retriever	Stream	Bicycle	Car
Monkey	Lemonade	Gown	Teacher	Map
Yacht	Telegraph pole	Politician	London	Tuesday

See if you can recall all 30 words, and where they went:

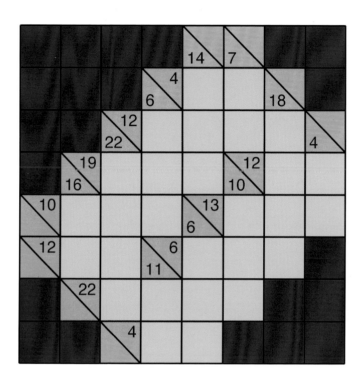

Kakuro

Fill in the grid so that each run of squares adds up to the total in the box above or to the left. You can only use the numbers 1 to 9, and you may not repeat any number within any run (a number may reoccur in the same row/column in a separate run). Totals below the diagonal line give the sum of the numbers in the run below, while totals to the right of the diagonal line give the sum of numbers in the run to the right.

No guessing is required, and there is only one solution. If you're not sure you understand the rules, then take a quick peek at the answer to see how it works.

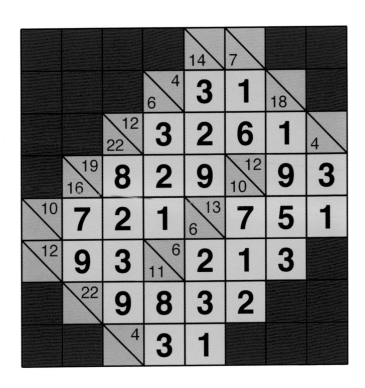

Which of these words is the odd one out, and why?
Earth   Moon   Wind   Fire   Water

Which number comes next in this sequence?
1   4   9   16   ?

Which of these words does not fit with the rest?
Levier   Relive   Virile   Revile

Which of these numbers is not a multiple of 5?
19,432,355   7,450   48,469   35,430

If I fall asleep at 10:30 p.m. and wake up at 6:15 p.m., how long have I been asleep?

If Sue drives at 60 mph for 10 minutes, then 30 mph for 10 minutes, followed by 70 mph for 6 minutes, how far does she travel in those 26 minutes?

If Sydney's summertime clock is 11 hours ahead of the UK while it's winter in the UK, how many hours ahead of the UK is Sydney when it's summer in the UK, given that both countries move their clocks forward an hour for the summer but back again in the winter?

Complete the following:
35% of 200 = ?   95% of 500 = ?   20% of 10% of 100 = ?

My sister's uncle's wife's daughter's brother is my cousin—true or false?

Which letter comes next in this sequence?
O T T F F S S ?

Complete the following:
50 − 60 + 30 = ?   99 − 199 + 299 = ?   3 x 7 x 5 = ?

If I press the button "4" on my mobile phone, I select G, then H, then I, while when I press "8," I get T, then U, then V. How many key presses do I need to type "THIGH"?

Which of these word pairs are not homophones? (Homophones are words that sound the same but are spelled differently).
Aural & Oral   Write & Right   Bread & Breed   Altar & Alter

True or false—if you put your right hand on your left ear and your left hand in your left pocket and then look in a mirror, you'll see that your right ear is being held by your left hand and your right hand is in your left pocket.

Which of these words is the odd one out, and why?

Earth   Moon   Wind   Fire   Water

Moon—only one that isn't an ancient element.

Which number comes next in this sequence?

1   4   9   16   ?

25. They are square numbers—i.e. 1x1=1, 2x2=4, 3x3=9, etc.

Which of these words does not fit with the rest?

Levier   Relive   Virile   Revile

Virile—the other three are anagrams of one another.

Which of these numbers is not a multiple of 5?

19,432,356   7,450   48,469   35,430

48,469.

If I fall asleep at 10:30 p.m. and wake up at 6:15 p.m., how long have I been asleep?

7 hours 45 minutes.

If Sue drives at 60 mph for 10 minutes, then 30 mph for 10 minutes, followed by 70 mph for 6 minutes, how far does she travel in those 26 minutes?

22 miles.

If Sydney's summertime clock is 11 hours ahead of the UK while it's winter in the UK, how many hours ahead of the UK is Sydney when it's summer in the UK, given that both countries move their clocks forward an hour for the summer but back again in the winter?

9 hours ahead.

Complete the following:

35% of 200 = ?   95% of 500 = ?   20% of 10% of 100 = ?

35% of 200 = 70   95% of 500 = 475   20% of 10% of 100 = 2

My sister's uncle's wife's daughter's brother is my cousin—true or false?

True.

Which letter comes next in this sequence?

O T T F F S S ?

E. They are the first letters of the numbers One, Two, Three, Four, etc.

Complete the following:

50 – 60 + 30 = ?   99 – 199 + 299 = ?   3 x 7 x 5 = ?

50 – 60 + 30 = 20   99 – 199 + 299 = 199   3 x 7 x 5 = 105

If I press the button "4" on my mobile phone, I select G, then H, then I, while when I press "8," I get T, then U, then V. How many key presses do I need to type "THIGH"?

9 key presses.

Which of these word pairs are not homophones? (Homophones are words that sound the same but are spelled differently).

Aural & Oral   Write & Right   Bread & Breed   Altar & Alter

Bread & Breed.

True or false—if you put your right hand on your left ear and your left hand in your left pocket and then look in a mirror, you'll see that your right ear is being held by your left hand and your right hand is in your left pocket.

False. It will appear your hand is in your right pocket.

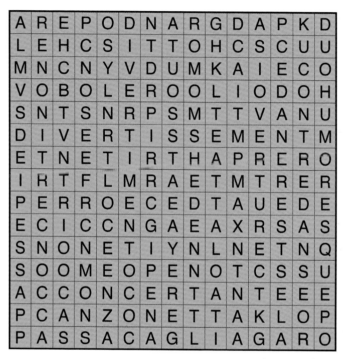

A	R	E	P	O	D	N	A	R	G	D	A	P	K	D
L	E	H	C	S	I	T	T	O	H	C	S	C	U	U
M	N	C	N	Y	V	D	U	M	K	A	I	E	C	O
V	O	B	O	L	E	R	O	O	L	I	O	D	O	H
S	N	T	S	N	R	P	S	M	T	T	V	A	N	U
D	I	V	E	R	T	I	S	S	E	M	E	N	T	M
E	T	N	E	T	I	R	T	H	A	P	R	E	R	O
I	R	T	F	L	M	R	A	E	T	M	T	R	E	R
P	E	R	R	O	E	C	E	D	T	A	U	E	D	E
E	C	I	C	C	N	G	A	E	A	X	R	S	A	S
S	N	O	N	E	T	I	Y	N	L	N	E	T	N	Q
S	O	O	M	E	O	P	E	N	O	T	C	S	S	U
A	C	C	O	N	C	E	R	T	A	N	T	E	E	E
P	C	A	N	Z	O	N	E	T	T	A	K	L	O	P
P	A	S	S	A	C	A	G	L	I	A	G	A	R	O

Try and find these musical movements within the grid.

BOLERO
CANON
CANZONETTA
CONCERTANTE
CONCERTINO
CONCERTSTIICK
CONTRADANCE
CONTREDANSEOR
DIVERTIMENTO
DIVERTISSEMENT
DUMKA

DUO
ELEGY
GRANDOPERA
HUMORESQUE
MASS
MOTET
NONET
OVERTURE
PASSACAGLIA
PASSEPIED
POLKA

PSALM
RAGA
REEL
SCHOTTISCHE
SERENADE
SEXTET
SINFONIETTA
STRATHSPEY
TONEPOEM
TRIO

		7	2	6	8	1		
	1				7		8	
							3	
		4	6					
	3	2				8	5	
					4	9		
	2							
	5		1				7	
		1	5	3	9	4		

Sudoku

Sudoku has one very simple rule: fill in the grid so that each row, column, and marked 3 by 3 box contains each of the numbers 1 to 9 once and once only.

No guessing is required, and there is only one solution. If you're not sure you understand the rules, then take a quick peek at the answer to see how it works.

3	9	7	2	6	8	1	4	5
5	1	6	3	4	7	2	8	9
2	4	8	9	1	5	6	3	7
9	8	4	6	5	3	7	1	2
6	3	2	7	9	1	8	5	4
1	7	5	8	2	4	9	6	3
8	2	3	4	7	6	5	9	1
4	5	9	1	8	2	3	7	6
7	6	1	5	3	9	4	2	8

Dave's decided to write some melodramatic poetry. It took him at least five minutes. See if it flows straight over you, or if you can remember anything about it once you've read it. Answer as many questions as you can without checking the poem again. Then when you've done that, go back and revisit the mellifluous melody of his meanderings and answer the rest.

REGRET

Seven months have softly flowed
Time has twisted, wound and weaved
Another year of absent crew
Left unchallenged. Run right through.

Nine and three the years untold
Wandered freely, flags unfurled.
Wind that doesn't wave the tree.
Losing nightly. Scaring me.

Flowers miss their springtime cheer
Waters boundless wait and ebb
Caught in pasts so deeply bound
Left behind. And never found.

Grasping hands have missed their bar
Muddled frenzies face the past
And chase it down, then turn away
Space engirdled. Wild affray.

Immolation wears the crown
Of fought and battled, torn and won
Lost and searching. Shorn of time
Sheep not cattle. No life, no rhyme.

- How many years does Dave describe as "untold"?
- How many verses are there in the poem?
- What body parts apparently missed their "bar"?
- What was wrong with springtime?
- How many verses start with a number?
- What was disturbing about the tree in Dave's poem?
- What animal is present instead of cattle?
- What period of time flowed softly?
- What was "boundless" and waiting?
- What is special about the last two lines of each verse?
- Something was unfurled—what was it?
- What did a "muddled frenzy" face?
- The final line of each verse always has how many full stops?
- At least how long did it take Dave to write the poem?
- What is the poem called?

How many years does Dave describe as "untold"?
Twelve years.

How many verses are there in the poem?
Five.

What body parts apparently missed their "bar"?
Hands.

What was wrong with springtime?
The flowers.

How many verses start with a number?
Two.

What was disturbing about the tree in Dave's poem?
The wind didn't affect it.

What animal is present instead of cattle?
Sheep.

What period of time flowed softly?
Seven months.

What was "boundless" and waiting?
Waters.

What is special about the last two lines of each verse?
They always rhyme.

Something was unfurled—what was it?
A flag.

What did a "muddled frenzy" face?
The past.

The final line of each verse always has how many full stops?
Two.

At least how long did it take Dave to write the poem?
Five minutes.

What is the poem called?
Regret.

```
·   ·   ·   ·   ·   ·   ·   ·   ·   ·
  2       3 1       2
· ·   ·   · ·   ·   ·   · ·   ·
3 3 2       3 1 1
· ·   · ·   ·   · ·   ·   ·   ·
          3       2 1 3
·   ·   ·   ·   ·   ·   ·   ·   ·   ·
3 2     1 2 0 1 3 2 2
· ·   ·   · ·   ·   · ·   · ·   ·
2     2       2   2 1
· ·   ·   ·   ·   · ·   ·   ·   ·
  1 2     2       2       2
· ·   ·   ·   · ·   ·   · ·   ·
3 2 2 2 2 1 3   1 2
· ·   · ·   · ·   ·   ·   ·   ·
2 3 2       2
· ·   ·   · ·   ·   ·   ·   ·   ·
  2 0 2           1 1 2
· ·   · ·   ·   · ·   · ·   ·
  3       2 3       3
·   · ·   ·   ·   ·   · ·   ·   ·
```

Slitherlink

Draw a single loop by connecting together the dots such that each numbered square has the specified number of adjacent line segments. You may only join dots by using straight horizontal or vertical lines, and the loop cannot cross or overlap itself in any way.
No guessing is required, and there is only one solution. If you're not sure you understand the rules, then take a quick peek at the answer to see how it works.

Kakuro

Fill in the grid so that each run of squares adds up to the total in the box above or to the left. You can only use the numbers 1 to 9, and you may not repeat any number within any run (a number may reoccur in the same row/column in a separate run). Totals below the diagonal line give the sum of the numbers in the run below, while totals to the right of the diagonal line give the sum of numbers in the run to the right.

No guessing is required, and there is only one solution. If you're not sure you understand the rules, then take a quick peek at the answer to see how it works.

Kakuro solution grid:

		27	29				6	3
	3	**1**	**2**			4 / 14	**3**	**1**
	12	**4**	**8**		12 / 25	**9**	**1**	**2**
	16 / 4	**9**	**7**	14	**9**	**3**	**2**	
20	**3**	**8**	**9**	3 / 11	**1**	**2**		
19	**1**	**5**	**3**	**2**	**8**	24	22	3
		27 / 11	**1**	**7**	**8**	**9**	**2**	
	5 / 14	**2**	**3**	7	**4**	**2**	**1**	
	22 / 11	**9**	**8**	**5**	4	**1**	**3**	
14	**9**	**4**	**1**		16	**9**	**7**	
3	**2**	**1**			3	**2**	**1**	

Which of these words is the odd one out, and why?
Trumpet   Clarinet   Trombone   French horn   Tuba

Which number comes next in this sequence?
1   3   9   27   81   ?

Can you find the connection between all these words?
Whine   Rhumb   Coax   Jinn

Think of a number. Add 26. Multiply by 90. Divide by 180. Multiply by 2. Subtract the number you thought of to start with. What number are you left with?

If every hour only had 50 minutes, how many minutes shorter would each day be?

If I drive at 30 mph for 6 minutes, then 60 mph for 10 minutes, followed by 30 mph for 4 minutes, what is my average speed over those 20 minutes?

To convert from Celsius (C) to Kelvin (K), you add 273. If it's 26°C outside right now, which is 9°K cooler than the hottest it's been today, what is today's hottest temperature in Kelvin?

Complete the following:
10% of 50% = ?   Half of a third of a quarter = ?   50 x 45 = ?

If an elephant never forgets and it learns 4 facts a day, how many facts does it learn in a 4-year period, assuming a leap year once every 4 years?

Which letter comes next in this pattern?
W L C N I T ?

Complete the following:
77 x 11 = ?   5 x 98 = ?   103 + 484 = ?

If a perfectly flat and square island has a surface area of 8100 square meters, how wide is the island?

How many of these words have more consonants than vowels?
Separately   Extremely   Confusing   Muddled   Failure

If I'm happy only 90% of the time, but when I sleep I'm always happy, what percentage of the time am I both awake and not happy?

Which of these words is the odd one out, and why?

Trumpet   Clarinet   Trombone   French horn   Tuba

Clarinet—only one that isn't a brass instrument.

Which number comes next in this sequence?

1   3   9   27   81   ?

243. Each number is 3 times the previous number.

Can you find the connection between all these words?

Whine   Rhumb   Coax   Jinn

They are all homophones of drinks—wine, rum, cokes, gin.

Think of a number. Add 26. Multiply by 90. Divide by 180. Multiply by 2. Subtract the number you thought of to start with. What number are you left with?

26—the rest of the sequence cancels itself out, so you don't need to do the math.

If every hour only had 50 minutes, how many minutes shorter would each day be?

240 minutes shorter.

If I drive at 30 mph for 6 minutes, then 60 mph for 10 minutes, followed by 30 mph for 4 minutes, what is my average speed over those 20 minutes?

I travel 3 miles, 10 miles, and 2 miles respectively in 20 minutes, so my average speed is 45 mph.

To convert from Celsius (C) to Kelvin (K), you add 273. If it's 26°C outside right now, which is 9°K cooler than the hottest it's been today, what is today's hottest temperature in Kelvin?

308°K.

Complete the following:

10% of 50% = ?   Half of a third of a quarter = ?   50 x 45 = ?

10% of 50% = 5%   Half of a third of a quarter = A twenty-fourth   50 x 45 = 2250

If an elephant never forgets and it learns 4 facts a day, how many facts does it learn in a 4-year period, assuming a leap year once every 4 years?

5844 facts. Clever elephant!

Which letter comes next in this pattern?

W L C N I T ?

P. They are the first letters of the words in the question!

Complete the following:

77 x 11 = ?   5 x 98 = ?   103 + 484 = ?

77 x 11 = 847   5 x 98 = 490   103 + 484 = 587

If a perfectly flat and square island has a surface area of 8100 square meters, how wide is the island?

90 meters wide.

How many of these words have more consonants than vowels?

Separately   Extremely   Confusing   Muddled   Failure

4—all of them except "failure."

If I'm happy only 90% of the time, but when I sleep I'm always happy, what percentage of the time am I both awake and not happy?

10% of the time.

Memory Test

This grid contains 30 types of government. On the next page see if you can recall where all 30 went—you will be given a list of the 30 types but all the boxes will be empty.

Heptarchy	Monarchy	Tyranny	Democracy	Constitutionalism
Ergatocracy	Absolutism	Communalism	Triarchy	Slavocracy
Squirearchy	Gerontocracy	Hierocracy	Meritocracy	Imperialism
Anarchy	Aristocracy	Plutocracy	Hexarchy	Isocracy
Oligarchy	Pantisocracy	Quangocracy	Technocracy	Hagiocracy
Dictatorship	Corporatism	Bureaucracy	Ochlocracy	Nomocracy

Try and put the governmental types back in the grid: (there's just one extra word added into the list that doesn't belong in any of the boxes)

Anarchy	absence of government
Aristocracy	by nobility
Absolutism	by an absolute ruler
Bureaucracy	by officials
Communalism	by self-governing communities
Corporatism	by corporations
Constitutionalism	by constitution
Dictatorship	by a dictator
Democracy	by the people
Ergatocracy	by the workers
Gerontocracy	by old people
Hierocracy	by priests
Hexarchy	by six rulers
Heptarchy	by seven rulers
Hagiocracy	by holy men
Isocracy	by equals
Imperialism	by emperor/empire
Meritocracy	by merit
Monarchy	by monarch
Nomocracy	by rule of law
Oligarchy	by the few
Ochlocracy	by mob
Pantisocracy	by all equally
Plutocracy	by the rich
Ptochocracy	by the poor
Quangocracy	by quangos
Squirearchy	by squires
Slavocracy	by slaveholders
Tyranny	by a tyrant
Technocracy	by experts
Triarchy	by three rulers

G	H	M	J	K	O	M	K	A	Y	A	P	A	P	M
H	U	I	A	X	R	A	A	I	L	O	N	G	A	M
A	A	M	C	H	O	A	H	E	M	L	O	C	K	T
W	P	A	A	K	O	B	B	E	B	B	I	R	C	H
T	R	R	R	N	O	G	G	R	A	N	A	N	A	B
H	I	O	A	I	G	R	A	P	E	F	R	U	I	T
O	C	B	N	C	A	R	Y	N	F	P	H	O	Y	E
R	O	U	D	N	O	V	O	I	Y	O	A	A	H	R
N	T	T	A	F	I	R	A	V	M	P	B	P	N	O
S	U	T	P	Y	L	A	C	U	E	L	A	L	E	M
A	E	E	A	I	C	A	C	A	G	A	L	U	D	A
N	I	R	O	N	W	O	O	D	M	R	O	M	N	C
D	E	N	I	P	D	O	O	W	E	S	O	R	I	Y
A	M	U	N	R	U	B	A	L	S	A	C	A	L	S
L	O	T	U	S	M	M	U	L	B	E	R	R	Y	U

Reach the peak of word search skill by finding these trees within the grid.

ACACIA	GUM	MELALEUCA
APRICOT	HAWTHORN	MULBERRY
BALSA	HEMLOCK	PAPAYA
BANANA	HICKORY	PAPERBARK
BAY	HORNBEAM	PINE
BIRCH	IRONWOOD	PLUM
BOX	JACARANDA	POMEGRANATE
BUTTERNUT	LABURNUM	POPLAR
COOLABAH	LINDEN	RAFFIA
CORKOAK	LOTUS	ROSEWOOD
EUCALYPTUS	MACROCARPA	SANDAL
FIR	MAGNOLIA	SYCAMORE
GRAPEFRUIT	MAHOGANY	
GUAVA	MANGROVE	

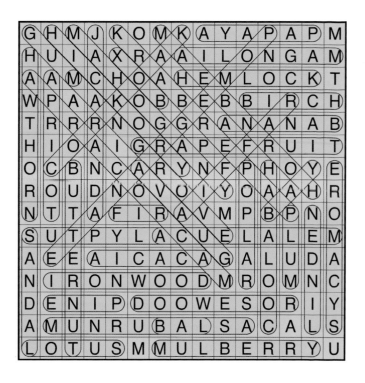

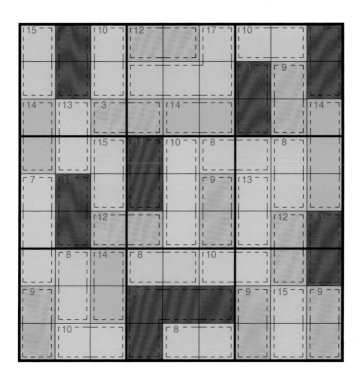

Killer Sudoku

Killer sudoku is a cross between Sudoku and Kakuro. Fill in the grid so that each row, column, and marked 3 by 3 box contains each of the numbers 1 to 9 once and once only. Additionally, you may not repeat a number within a dashed-line shape and numbers must be placed such that the total of the numbers in each dashed-line shape is equal to the number at the top-left of that shape.

No guessing is required, and there is only one solution. If you're not sure you understand the rules, then take a quick peek at the answer to see how it works.

8	2	4	5	7	3	9	1	6
7	3	6	4	9	1	8	2	5
5	9	1	2	6	8	3	7	4
9	4	7	8	5	6	2	3	1
1	6	8	3	4	2	7	5	9
2	5	3	9	1	7	6	4	8
4	7	5	6	2	9	1	8	3
3	1	9	7	8	4	5	6	2
6	8	2	1	3	5	4	9	7

Which of these words is the odd one out, and why?
Apple   Orange   Cherry   Fig   Tomato

Sort these numbers into the alphabetical order of their corresponding words:
1   2   4   5   3   9

What number comes next in this sequence?
31   28   31   30   ?

If the printer sends me 10% more business cards than I ordered, and after a year I have 25% left of those I had received from the printer, how many did I order originally if I now have 275 cards left?

Given that a millisecond is a thousandth of a second, how many milliseconds are there in a minute?

If I drive the 40 miles from Cardiff to Swansea at 60 mph, but my friend catches the train that takes a 30-mile route but stops at lots of stations and goes an average of only 40 mph, who will arrive first if we both leave at the same time?

If the hottest country in the world today is Egypt, which is twice as hot in degrees Celsius as Japan, which in turn is three times hotter than Greenland, how hot is it in Iceland if it's three degrees cooler than a fifth of the temperature of Greenland and it's thirty Celsius in Egypt?

Complete the following:
0.5 x 25 = ?   50 x 35 = ?   80 x 700 = ?

If somebody born on March 13, 1878, died on January 2, 1953, how many birthdays had they celebrated by the time they died?

Which letter comes next in this pattern?
A S D F G ?

Complete the following:
Half of 80% of a third of 300 = ?   9 x 8 x 7 x 6 x 4 x 2 = ?

What is the sum of all numbers less than 50 that contain the digit "1"?

How many of these words have less consonants than vowels?
Three   Five   Twenty   Seven   Four   Six

This book has 15 multiple-question puzzle pages, and this is the 14th of them. However, of these 14, I haven't completed half yet, so how many do I still have left to complete in total?

Which of these words is the odd one out, and why?

| Apple | Orange | Cherry | Fig | Tomato |

Tomato—only one that doesn't grow on a tree.

Sort these numbers into the alphabetical order of their corresponding words:

| 1 | 2 | 4 | 5 | 3 | 9 |

5, 4, 9, 1, 3, 2. Five, Four, Nine, One, Three, Two.

What number comes next in this sequence?

| 31 | 28 | 31 | 30 | ? |

31. Number of days normally in January, February, March, etc.

If the printer sends me 10% more business cards than I ordered, and after a year I have 25% left of those I had received from the printer, how many did I order originally if I now have 275 cards left?

1,000 cards.

Given that a millisecond is a thousandth of a second, how many milliseconds are there in a minute?

60,000 milliseconds.

If I drive the 40 miles from Cardiff to Swansea at 60 mph, but my friend catches the train that takes a 30-mile route but stops at lots of stations and goes an average of only 40 mph, who will arrive first if we both leave at the same time?

My car journey takes 40 minutes, but my friend's train journey takes 45 minutes. So I arrive first.

If the hottest country in the world today is Egypt, which is twice as hot in degrees Celsius as Japan, which in turn is three times hotter than Greenland, how hot is it in Iceland if it's three degrees cooler than a fifth of the temperature of Greenland and it's thirty Celsius in Egypt?

-2°C in Iceland.

Complete the following:

0.5 x 25 = ?   50 x 35 = ?   80 x 700 = ?

0.5 x 25 = 12.5   50 x 35 = 1750   80 x 700 = 56000

If somebody born on March 13, 1878, died on January 2, 1953, how many birthdays had they celebrated by the time they died?

74 birthdays.

Which letter comes next in this pattern?

A S D F G ?

H. They are the letters on a standard QWERTY keyboard, reading from left to right on the middle row.

Complete the following:

Half of 80% of a third of 300 = ?   9 x 8 x 7 x 6 x 4 x 2 = ?

Half of 80% of a third of 300 = 40   9 x 8 x 7 x 6 x 4 x 2 = 24192

What is the sum of all numbers less than 50 that contain the digit "1"?

239. (1 + 10 + 11 + . . . + 18 + 19 + 21 + 31 + 41)

How many of these words have fewer consonants than vowels?

| Three | Five | Twenty | Seven | Four | Six |

None of them!

This book has 15 multiple-question puzzle pages, and this is the 14th of them. However, of these 14, I haven't completed half yet, so how many do I still have left to complete in total?

8.

Kakuro

Fill in the grid so that each run of squares adds up to the total in the box above or to the left. You can only use the numbers 1 to 9, and you may not repeat any number within any run (a number may reoccur in the same row/column in a separate run). Totals below the diagonal line give the sum of the numbers in the run below, while totals to the right of the diagonal line give the sum of numbers in the run to the right.

No guessing is required, and there is only one solution. If you're not sure you understand the rules, then take a quick peek at the answer to see how it works.

■	■	■	■	■	13\	11\	■	■	■
■	■	■	■	12\4	1	3	■	■	■
■	■	■	6\12	1	3	8	■	11\	4\
■	■	20\20	3	8	9	■	24\4	3	1
■	9\14	9	2	3	■	7\18	7	8	3
\12	3	8	1	■	24\11	2	9	20\	10\
\3	1	2	13\	7\23	9	1	8	3	2
\23	5	1	3	2	8	4	\5	1	4
■	6\	19\10	2	1	7	■	6\3	2	1
\23	3	9	7	4	■	20\9	1	5	3
\10	2	7	1	■	11\15	4	2	9	■
\4	1	3	■	3\19	7	9	3	■	■
■	■	■	\11	1	3	7	■	■	■
■	■	■	\3	2	1	■	■	■	■

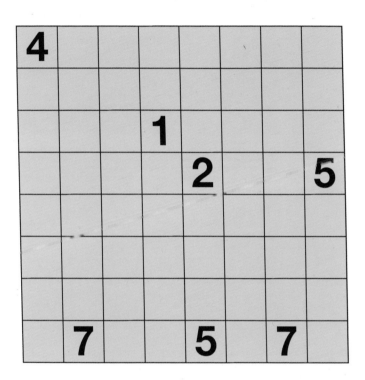

Nurikabe

Shade in squares in the grid in order to leave each number in a continuous unshaded area of the stated number of squares, bounded by shaded squares. Unshaded areas cannot touch in either a horizontal or vertical direction. All shaded squares must form a single continuous area, and there must be no 2x2 blocks of shaded squares.

No guessing is required, and there is only one solution. If you're not sure you understand the rules, then take a quick peek at the answer to see how it works.

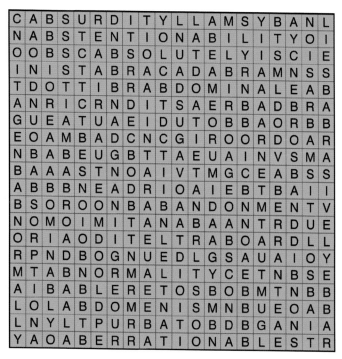

C	A	B	S	U	R	D	I	T	Y	L	L	A	M	S	Y	B	A	N	L
N	A	B	S	T	E	N	T	I	O	N	A	B	I	L	I	T	Y	O	I
O	O	B	S	C	A	B	S	O	L	U	T	E	L	Y	I	S	C	I	E
I	N	I	S	T	A	B	R	A	C	A	D	A	B	R	A	M	N	S	S
T	D	O	T	T	I	B	R	A	B	D	O	M	I	N	A	L	E	A	B
A	N	R	I	C	R	N	D	I	T	S	A	E	R	B	A	D	B	R	A
G	U	E	A	T	U	A	E	I	D	U	T	O	B	B	A	O	R	B	B
E	O	A	M	B	A	D	C	N	C	G	I	R	O	O	R	D	O	A	R
N	B	A	B	E	U	G	B	T	T	A	E	U	A	I	N	V	S	M	A
B	A	A	A	S	T	N	O	A	I	V	T	M	G	C	E	A	B	S	S
A	B	B	B	N	E	A	D	R	I	O	A	I	E	B	T	B	A	I	I
B	S	O	R	O	O	N	B	A	B	A	N	D	O	N	M	E	N	T	V
N	O	M	O	I	M	I	T	A	N	A	B	A	A	N	T	R	D	U	E
O	R	I	A	O	D	I	T	E	L	T	R	A	B	O	A	R	D	L	L
R	P	N	D	B	O	G	N	U	E	D	L	G	S	A	U	A	I	O	Y
M	T	A	B	N	O	R	M	A	L	I	T	Y	C	E	T	N	B	S	E
A	I	B	A	B	L	E	R	E	T	O	S	B	O	B	M	T	N	B	B
L	O	L	A	B	D	O	M	E	N	I	S	M	N	B	U	E	O	A	B
L	N	Y	L	T	P	U	R	B	A	T	O	B	D	B	G	A	N	I	A
Y	A	O	A	B	E	R	R	A	T	I	O	N	A	B	L	E	S	T	R

Find all these AB words in the grid—if you're able!

ABANDONMENT
ABASEMENT
ABATEMENT
ABATTOIR
ABBEY
ABBOT
ABBREVIATION
ABDICATION
ABDOMEN
ABDOMINAL
ABDUCTION
ABERRANT
ABERRATION
ABILITY
ABLER
ABLEST
ABNEGATION

ABNORMALITY
ABNORMALLY
ABOARD
ABOMINABLY
ABOMINATION
ABORIGINAL
ABOUND
ABOUT
ABOVEBOARD
ABRACADABRA
ABRASION
ABRASIVELY
ABREAST
ABRIDGEMENT
ABRIDGMENT
ABROAD
ABROGATION

ABRUPTLY
ABSCOND
ABSEIL
ABSENTEEISM
ABSOLUTELY
ABSOLUTION
ABSOLUTISM
ABSORBENCY
ABSORPTION
ABSTENTION
ABSTINENT
ABSTRACTEDLY
ABSTRACTION
ABSURDITY
ABUNDANTLY
ABUT
ABYSMALLY

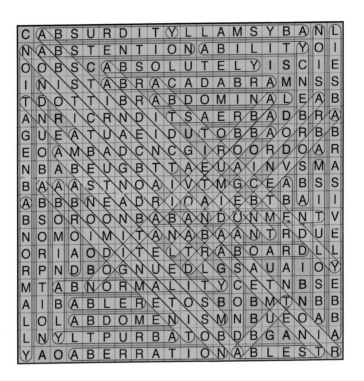

Memory Test

Try and remember where these 24 historical characters fit in the grid, then write them back in on the next page. You will be given very little help.

Alexander the Great	Martin Luther	Mahatma Gandhi	Socrates
Marco Polo	Napoleon Bonaparte	Geronimo	George Washington
Boudicca	Guy Fawkes	Attila the Hun	Henry VIII
Billy the Kid	Leon Trotsky	Robert the Bruce	Joseph Stalin
Winston Churchill	Horatio Nelson	Julius Caesar	Charlemagne
Davy Crockett	Walter Raleigh	Yuri Gagarin	Florence Nightingale

Now try and write them back in:

	M		
		G	
			H
B			
	H		
	W		

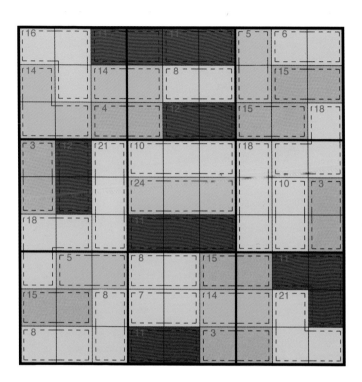

Killer Sudoku

Killer sudoku is a cross between Sudoku and Kakuro. Fill in the grid so that each row, column, and marked 3 by 3 box contains each of the numbers 1 to 9 once and once only. Additionally, you may not repeat a number within a dashed-line shape and numbers must be placed such that the total of the numbers in each dashed-line shape is equal to the number at the top-left of that shape.

No guessing is required, and there is only one solution. If you're not sure you understand the rules, then take a quick peek at the answer to see how it works.

6	9	7	4	8	3	2	1	5
4	1	5	9	2	6	3	8	7
8	2	3	1	7	5	9	6	4
2	7	8	3	6	1	4	5	9
1	5	4	8	9	7	6	3	2
3	6	9	2	5	4	8	7	1
9	4	1	5	3	8	7	2	6
7	8	2	6	1	9	5	4	3
5	3	6	7	4	2	1	9	8

```
.   .   .   .   .   .   .   .   .   .
  1 . 2   . 1 . 2 . 3   . 2   .   .
.     . 3     .     . 1   . 2   .   .
. 2   . 0   . 1 . 3     .     .   2 .
. 2 . 2 . 3 . 2   .   . 0 . 2 . 2 . 1 .
. 1   . 2     .   . 1   .     .     .
.   .   . 2   .   .   . 2   . 1 .
. 3 . 2 . 3 . 1   .   . 2 . 2 . 3 . 3 .
. 1   .   . 2 . 3   . 3   . 2 .
.   . 2   . 2   .   . 2   .   .
.   . 1   . 3 . 3 . 3   . 1 . 2   .   .
.   .   .   .   .   .   .   .   .   .
```

Slitherlink

Draw a single loop by connecting together the dots such that each numbered square has the specified number of adjacent line segments. You may only join dots by using straight horizontal or vertical lines, and the loop cannot cross or overlap itself in any way.

No guessing is required, and there is only one solution. If you're not sure you understand the rules, then take a quick peek at the answer to see how it works.

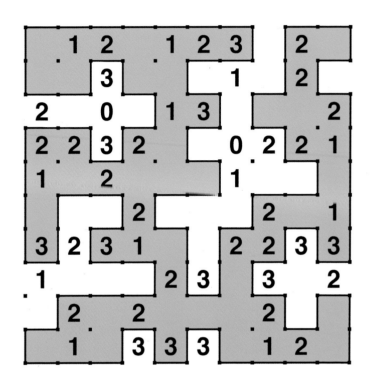

S	A	M	O	A	R	G	E	N	T	I	N	A	I	N	A	Z	N	A	T
A	L	E	U	Z	E	N	E	V	A	E	U	Q	I	B	M	A	Z	O	M
U	A	I	S	E	N	O	D	N	I	P	A	K	I	S	T	A	N	E	P
G	M	G	R	R	S	E	Y	C	H	E	L	L	E	S	K	O	R	E	A
A	E	U	Z	B	E	K	I	S	T	A	N	S	H	U	P	O	B	A	L
R	T	E	N	A	T	S	Z	Y	G	R	Y	K	V	R	P	I	O	I	A
A	A	R	K	I	M	A	U	R	I	T	A	N	I	A	P	S	T	S	U
C	U	N	S	J	E	U	R	E	P	Z	U	I	G	C	L	H	S	S	A
I	G	S	D	A	T	T	I	R	A	Q	O	N	L	S	U	D	W	U	I
N	C	E	N	N	K	R	S	K	E	G	I	B	R	A	L	T	A	R	N
E	P	Y	A	F	G	H	A	N	I	S	T	A	N	G	R	E	N	R	O
P	H	I	L	I	P	P	I	N	E	S	T	I	M	A	L	T	A	M	D
A	T	U	R	K	M	E	N	I	S	T	A	N	N	D	M	L	S	A	E
L	U	X	E	M	B	O	U	R	G	N	H	S	O	A	A	I	Z	U	C
E	R	F	H	A	K	R	O	T	I	R	I	C	N	M	U	H	B	R	A
S	K	I	T	A	B	I	R	I	K	A	I	S	E	N	O	R	C	I	M
T	E	J	E	I	T	D	N	A	L	R	E	Z	T	I	W	S	U	T	A
I	Y	I	N	A	T	S	I	K	I	J	A	T	T	R	L	E	U	I	N
N	D	N	A	L	I	L	A	M	O	S	A	F	A	N	I	K	R	U	B
E	T	H	I	O	P	I	A	H	S	E	D	A	L	G	N	A	B	S	C

These countries are all hidden within the grid—seek them out!

AFGHANISTAN
AKROTIRI
ARGENTINA
AUSTRALIA
AZERBAIJAN
BANGLADESH
BOTSWANA
BURKINAFASO
CHAD
ETHIOPIA
FIJI
GIBRALTAR
GUATEMALA
GUERNSEY
INDONESIA
IRAQ
KAZAKHSTAN
KIRIBATI
KOREA

KYRGYZSTAN
LIECHTENSTEIN
LITHUANIA
LUXEMBOURG
MACEDONIA
MADAGASCAR
MALTA
MAURITANIA
MAURITIUS
MICRONESIA
MONTSERRAT
MOZAMBIQUE
NAMIBIA
NAURU
NEPAL
NETHERLANDS
NICARAGUA
NIUE
PAKISTAN

PALAU
PALESTINE
PERU
PHILIPPINES
RUSSIA
SAMOA
SEYCHELLES
SINGAPORE
SOMALILAND
SPAIN
SVALBARD
SWITZERLAND
TAJIKISTAN
TANZANIA
TRANSNISTRIA
TURKEY
TURKMENISTAN
UZBEKISTAN
VENEZUELA

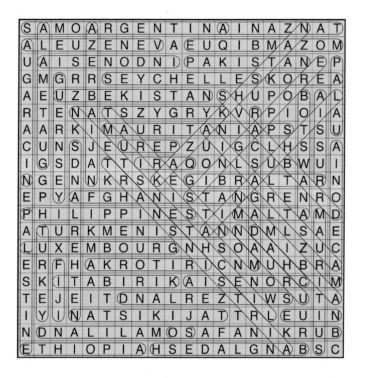

Kakuro

Fill in the grid so that each run of squares adds up to the total in the box above or to the left. You can only use the numbers 1 to 9, and you may not repeat any number within any run (a number may reoccur in the same row/column in a separate run). Totals below the diagonal line give the sum of the numbers in the run below, while totals to the right of the diagonal line give the sum of numbers in the run to the right.

No guessing is required, and there is only one solution. If you're not sure you understand the rules, then take a quick peek at the answer to see how it works.

	11\	13\	9\	17\		10\	21\		
\10	3	4	2	1	\16	7	9	33\	16\
\26	8	9	7	2	16\24	2	6	9	7
	5\	23\	\30	3	7	1	2	8	9
\4	1	3	29\14	5	9	18\10	3	7	13\
\27	4	8	9	6	17\10	2	1	3	4
	9\6	1	5	3\17	9	8	\15	6	9
\25	3	4	7	2	8	1	14\	27\	17\
\22	6	7	8	1	16\16	4	2	1	9
	16\	25\		11\25	9	3	1	4	8
\8	7	1	11\12	5	7	21\14	5	9	4\
\26	9	8	3	6	9\22	5	6	8	3
	\16	9	7	\9	2	7	\6	5	1
	\8	7	1	\16	7	9			

Which of these words is the odd one out, and why?
Carbon   Hydrogen   Helium   Bronze   Copper

Which number comes next in this sequence?
1   10   11   100   101?

Which of these words is the odd one out, and why?
Run   Skip   Walk   Roll   Jog

Which of these numbers is the odd one out?
351   423   711   262   180

How many seconds are there in half a week?

If the Cambridge to London express train leaves Cambridge at 10:30 a.m. and travels an average of 90 mph, while the slower non-express train for the same route leaves at 10:15 a.m. but travels at an average of 60 mph, how many minutes sooner will the express train arrive in London, given that the distance traveled is 60 miles?

If global warming causes the height of the oceans to rise by 1 cm for every half a degree Celsius rise in average temperature, and if in 40 years the temperature has risen an average of 5 Celsius, then by how much will the oceans have risen?

Complete the following:
123 + 456 + 789 = ?   963 x 3 = ?   145 x 5 = ?

True or false? Tuesday is the day after Monday if you order the days of the week alphabetically.

Which letter comes next in this pattern?
J F M A M J J ?

Complete the following:
80% of 120 = ?   2 x 58275 x 0.5 = ?   78% of 100% of 200 = ?

If I have just four matching pairs of gloves in a drawer, how many gloves do I need to pull out of the drawer before I am sure of having two matching pairs?

If I toss a coin six times, what is the probability that I guess heads or tails correctly all six times?

I'm feeling lucky, so I bet $50 on "red" at a casino. Given that there are the numbers 0 to 36 on the board, of which 18 are red, am I more or less or equally likely to win my bet than to guess the result of a single coin toss?

Which of these words is the odd one out, and why?

Carbon Hydrogen Helium Bronze Copper

Bronze—only one that isn't an element.

Which number comes next in this sequence?

1 10 11 100 101 ?

110. It is 1, 2, 3, 4, 5, 6 in binary.

Which of these words is the odd one out, and why?

Run Skip Walk Roll Jog

Roll—only one that doesn't always involve using your legs to move.

Which of these numbers is the odd one out?

351 423 711 262 180

262—the only one whose digits don't add up to to 9.

How many seconds are there in half a week?

302,400 seconds.

If the Cambridge to London express train leaves Cambridge at 10:30 a.m. and travels an average of 90 mph, while the slower non-express train for the same route leaves at 10:15 a.m. but travels at an average of 60 mph, how many minutes sooner will the express train arrive in London, given that the distance traveled is 60 miles?

The express train arrives 5 minutes sooner. The express takes 40 minutes and arrives at 11:10 a.m.; the slow train takes an hour and arrives at 11:15 a.m.

If global warming causes the height of the oceans to rise by 1 cm for every half a degree Celsius rise in average temperature, and if in 40 years the temperature has risen an average of 5 Celsius, then by how much will the oceans have risen?

10 cm.

Complete the following:

123 + 456 + 789 = ?   963 x 3 = ?   145 x 5 = ?

123 + 456 + 789 = 1368   963 x 3 = 2889   145 x 5 = 725

True or false? Tuesdays are the day after Monday if you order the days of the week alphabetically?

False. The day after Monday would be Saturday.

Which letter comes next in this pattern?

J F M A M J J ?

A. They are the first letters of the months of the year: January, February, etc.

Complete the following:

80% of 120 = ?   2 x 58275 x 0.5 = ?   78% of 100% of 200 = ?

80% of 120 = 96   2 x 58275 x 0.5 = 58275   78% of 100% of 200 = 156

If I have just four matching pairs of gloves in a drawer, how many gloves do I need to pull out of the drawer before I am sure of having two matching pairs?

6.

If I toss a coin six times, what is the probability that I guess heads or tails correctly all six times?

1 in 64. (1 in 2 multiplied by itself six times).

I'm feeling lucky, so I bet $50 on "red" at a casino. Given that there are the numbers 0 to 36 on the board, of which 18 are red, am I more or less or equally likely to win my bet than to guess the result of a single coin toss?

I'm less likely to win—with the 0 there are a total of 37 numbers on the casino board so my 18 in 37 chance is less than 1 in 2, while the likelihood of guessing a coin toss is precisely 1 in 2.